TAXATION AND SUITABILITY OF ANNUITIES
FOR THE PROFESSIONAL ADVISOR

John L. Olsen, CLU, ChFC, AEP

This book is for educational purposes only and does not provide legal, tax, or investment advice. Readers should consult their own advisor for their personal situation. Any laws or regulations cited have been edited and summarized for clarity's sake. Any names used in this publication are fictional and have no relationship to any person living or dead. Information is from sources believed accurate but is not warranted.

©2012 by John Olsen
Published by Olsen & Marrion, LLC.

All rights reserved. The text of this publication, or any part thereof, may not be reproduced in any manner whatsoever without written permission from the publisher.

Printed in the United States of America

First Printing, December 2012

ISBN   0-9728251-4-2

Olsen & Marrion, LLC   (314) 255-6531
2187 Butterfield Court
St. Louis MO 63043   info@indexannuitybook.com

This work is dedicated to my wife, Katherine, without whose unflagging support I would never have begun my first book, much less finished this one.

Acknowledgments:

No book is ever constructed entirely by its author. In writing this one, I have been helped greatly by many people. My partner, Jack Marrion, made the final product look far better than the drafts I sent him. Gary Underwood and Bruce Tannahill shared their knowledge of the often bewildering rules of annuity taxation. Dick Weber and Ben Baldwin, fellow members of the Society of Financial Service Professionals' Fiduciary Duty Committee, helped me to understand the implications of the regulatory announcements discussed. Michael Kitces (my co-author of *The Annuity Advisor*) was of invaluable help to me (as always). I am also grateful for the contributions and encouragement of Stephanie Curry, Mary Ann Mancini, Mel Warshaw, Ralph Spaulding, and April Caudill. If I've forgotten someone (which, given the present state of my memory, is quite likely), I ask forgiveness.

- John Olsen

TAXATION AND SUITABILITY OF ANNUITIES FOR THE PROFESSIONAL ADVISOR

Chapter 1: Annuity Basics	1
Chapter 2: Taxation of Annuities During Lifetime	21
Chapter Three: Taxation of Annuities After Death	45
Chapter Four: Annuities and Trusts	67
Chapter 5: Suitability and Annuities	77
Annuities and Suitability: Reflections on the State of the Debate	101
Index	118

FOREWARD

This book was written for attorneys, accountants, trust officers, financial advisors, and anyone else who may be called upon to render advice as to how annuities are taxed and when they may, under current rules at least, be considered appropriate. It is intended to be a general overview and not an exhaustive treatment. To the best of the author's knowledge and belief, the information contained is correct and the interpretations made are reasonable. However, the author offers no guarantees on either score. Readers are urged to consult their own tax counsel.

For many years, the author has served as an expert witness in court and arbitration cases involving annuity sales. Sometimes, such cases are brought against an advisor who recommended an annuity that was unsuitable (or structured unsuitably) for the purchaser, but who did not do so intentionally. *He or she simply didn't know enough about when annuities are or are not appropriate and how they're taxed to avoid making a bad recommendation.*

This book is intended to help the reader avoid that condition. If its content seems, at times, dry and hard to swallow (and it will seem so), think of it as preventive medicine.

Chapter 1: Annuity Basics

At one time or another, nearly every financial, tax, trust, or legal advisor will be called upon to deal with, and perhaps make recommendations regarding, an annuity contract. This can often present problems for those unfamiliar with these instruments and the complicated tax rules that govern them. In this chapter, we will examine the various types of annuities and some common "riders" (optional provisions attached to the contracts).

Let's begin by defining our terms. The term "annuity" can be confusing, as it is often used to describe both a series of payments over time and the contract from which those payments are paid. Strictly speaking, the latter usage should define an "annuity contract" (that is "a financial instrument where a premium is paid to a company or, in some cases, an individual in return for a promise to pay a certain amount for either a specific period of time, or over the lifetime of an individual")[1]. By contrast, the term "annuity" refers (in the strictest sense) to "all periodic payments resulting from the systematic liquidation of a principal sum and refers not only to payments for a life or lives, but also to installment payments that do not involve life contingency; for example, payments under a "fixed period" or "fixed amount" settlement option"[2].

That said, the word "annuity", in common parlance, refers to the contract, rather than to the payments, and we will employ that usage in this book (i.e.: "annuity" = "annuity contract"), except when we're discussing "amounts received as an annuity", a term of art used *only* to describe certain payments from an annuity contract.

There are several kinds of annuity contracts - e.g.: *private annuities, charitable gift annuities, and commercial annuities* – but we will confine our discussion to the last, and most common, type – *commercial annuities*. A commercial annuity is a contract between an issuer (generally, an insurance company) and a buyer which guarantees that buyer the right to receive an *income* (a series of payments) over a specified period or for the lifetime(s) of one or more *"annuitants"*. Moreover, in our review of annuity taxation, we will be considering only "*non-qualified*" contracts - commercial annuities that are purchased *outside*

Chapter 1: Annuity Basics

IRAs or qualified plans – because the tax rules that govern annuities inside such plans are, with very few exceptions, identical to those applicable to other investments held in those plans.

Types of Commercial Annuities

It is possible to divide all annuities into two types – but one must do this twice, from two different perspectives – in terms of when annuity payments will begin and in terms of how the contract value will be invested.

When Payments Become Payable: Immediate vs. Deferred

An *immediate annuity* is one in which regular annuity payments *must* commence within one year of the date of issue. A *deferred annuity* is one in which payments *may* (but not necessarily must) be deferred – possibly indefinitely.

How Contract Value Is Invested: Fixed vs. Variable

The Fixed Annuity

A *fixed annuity* may be either immediate or deferred. Contrary to popular belief, the term "fixed" in "fixed annuity" *does not* refer to the interest crediting (because the prospective *non-guaranteed* - or "excess" – interest credited to these contracts will be whatever the issuing insurer declares it to be, usually on an annual basis), but, rather to the fact that the contract value is expressed in units that are fixed in value – dollars.

The Fixed Immediate Annuity

A *fixed immediate annuity* pays an income that is fixed in amount (either level or increasing at a constant rate, chosen at issue by the purchaser[3]). The income will persist for a specified period of years (a "period certain" annuity) or for the lifetime of the annuitant (a "life contingent" annuity) A life contingent annuity may provide for a "refund feature", an amount guaranteed to be paid to the beneficiary if the annuitant dies before a specified number of years or before the amount annuitized has been entirely paid out as income.

The Fixed Deferred Annuity

A *fixed deferred annuity* is one in which the accumulation value will never decrease (except through distributions) and will increase by the crediting of interest. All fixed deferred annuities guarantee both principal and a minimum interest crediting rate. Additional, non-guaranteed interest may be declared, each year, by the issuing insurer. The contract may be *annuitized* (that is, placed under an annuity payout option), usually after the first year. An annuitized deferred annuity acts like, and is taxed like, an immediate annuity.

The Fixed "Indexed" Annuity

A variation of the fixed deferred annuity is the *indexed annuity*, in which interest to be credited is linked to the performance of a published index (usually, but not always, the S&P500). *As of this writing, all indexed annuities are of the deferred type.* An indexed annuity is *not* a "third type of contract"; it is a *fixed* annuity because (a) its value is expressed in terms of fixed units (in this country, U.S. dollars) and (b) because it provides guarantees of principal and minimum interest.

The Variable Annuity

A *variable* annuity is one in which the value is measured in terms of units that can, and usually will, vary from day to day, depending upon the performance of the investment accounts chosen by the purchaser. Like a fixed annuity, a variable annuity can be either immediate or deferred.

The Variable Immediate Annuity

In a *variable immediate annuity*, the value of each year's annuity payment will vary in amount, reflecting the performance of the investment accounts chosen and will persist either for life or for a period of years (as with the fixed immediate annuity).

The Variable Deferred Annuity

In a *variable deferred annuity*, there is no guarantee of principal or of a minimum rate of return (except for money placed in the "fixed account" of the annuity). The contract value is expressed in terms of *units* that vary in value, according to the performance of the chosen investment accounts (often referred to either as "separate accounts" or "sub-accounts"). As with a fixed deferred annuity, the variable deferred annuity has two "phases":

The Accumulation Phase extends from the contract purchase date to the date on which the contract is "annuitized" (that is, placed under a regular annuity payout option). Most deferred annuities (fixed or variable) specify a *maturity date* by which the contract must either be surrendered or annuitized. Many contracts permit the owner to extend that date (usually to a maximum age of 85-95). Some misinformed critics of annuities have suggested that if an annuity has a maturity date of owner's age 85, this means that the owner cannot "get at" the money in the annuity until that age. That is totally false. *All* deferred annuity contracts permit the owner to annuitize after an initial waiting period (often one year, and rarely later than the fifth year).

The "Annuity Phase" (or "Payout Phase") extends from the date of annuitization until the later of the last annuitant's death or the expiry of the "guarantee period" (if that period extends beyond the death of the last annuitant).

In the "annuity" phase, a deferred annuity contract performs like, and is taxed

> The "maturity date" of a deferred annuity is **not** the earliest point at which the owner can access contract values. It is the date by which the contract must be either surrendered or annuitized. Contract values may be accessed by means of partial withdrawals, and annuitization is generally available at any time after the first year (or, in some contracts, after the first few years).

exactly like, an immediate annuity. In fixed contracts, the amount of each annuity payment is either fixed in amount or will increase at a pre-determined rate (often called the "COLA" [Cost of Living] rate). In variable deferred annuity contracts (as in variable immediate annuities), the amount of each year's annuity payment will depend upon the performance of the underlying investments. For a more detailed discussion of how variable annuity payments are calculated, see Olsen & Kitces, *The Advisor's Guide to Annuities*, (National Underwriter Co., 3rd ed., 2012).

Parties to the Contract

There are four parties to a commercial annuity contract.

1. The *Insurance company* that issued the contract is responsible for keeping all the promises therein.

2. The *owner* is the individual or entity that owns the contract and can make decisions regarding it.

3. The *annuitant* is the individual (it must be a human being) whose age and sex (for sex-distinct annuities) determine the amount of the annuity income. Contrary to popular belief, the annuitant is *not* the individual who will receive the annuity benefit unless he/she is also the owner or the owner has directed payment to the beneficiary. The annuitant may or may not be the same individual as the owner; when this is not the case, problems may arise, as we'll see in our review of annuity taxation.

4. The *beneficiary* is the party that will receive a death benefit if the annuity provides for one. But *whose death* will trigger payment and *which death benefit* will be payable upon that death depends upon the contract (as discussed in Chapter 3 – Taxation of Annuities after Death).

Types of Annuity Payout Arrangements

An annuity may be structured to provide income payments either for a period of years or for the lifetime(s) of one or more annuitants.

The "Period Certain" Annuity

The "Period Certain" annuity guarantees annuity payments for a certain period of time (e.g.: ten years). The amount of each annuity payment *does not* depend upon the life expectancy of the annuitant, and payments will persist for the entire period even if the annuitant does not survive it. The Period Certain payout arrangement is used both in immediate annuities (in which payments will commence within one year of purchase and will persist for the period chosen) and as a payout option from a deferred annuity. In the latter case, income payments will commence at the *Annuity Starting Date* (ASD) and will persist for the period chosen.

The "Life Contingent" Annuity

The "Life Contingent" (or "Life") annuity is a payout option, either from an immediate annuity or from a deferred annuity that the owner has elected to annuitize, that will persist for the lifetime(s) of one or more annuitants. There are several types of Life Contingent annuity payouts.

"Life Only" (or "Straight Life") Annuity Payout

A "Life Only" annuity guarantees to make annuity payments for the life of one or more annuitants. If only one annuitant is named, payments cease (and the contract expires) upon that individual's death, regardless of when that occurs. If more than one annuitant is named, payments cease upon the death of the last annuitant.

In the author's experience, this arrangement is rarely elected, possibly because most purchasers are unwilling to 'let the insurance company keep" any unpaid contract value should they die "early".

While this perception is certainly understandable, it is incorrect, as the insurance company does not "keep the money", but, rather, uses it to make payments to annuitants of other contracts who have not "died early". The essential principle behind annuity (and life insurance) contracts is *"risk pooling"*. The amount of annuity payments is based, not only how long an individual annuitant will actually live (which is unknowable), but upon *average* life expectancies. In a pool of "life only" annuitants, some will die before life expectancy and others will live longer. Annuity payout rates are calculated to permit the insurer to make benefit payments to all annuitants in the pool.

The "Life Only" annuity will *always* provide a higher benefit than one which provides a "refund feature" (a guarantee of a minimum payout if the annuitant dies "early"). A "Life Only" *fixed* annuity *always* provides – to *any* annuitant- a higher level of guaranteed income for life than can be obtained from *any* other financial instrument, because of the *"mortality credit"* (the actuarial certainty that *some* annuitants will die after receiving only a few payments, and that the undistributed value from their contracts will be available to make payments to the remaining annuitants in the risk pool) incorporated in annuity payout rates.

That said, few consumers elect this payout arrangement. As the author observed in *The Annuity Advisor*, "life only" annuities are usually purchased only by two groups of individuals- those who have no heirs, and those who dislike their heirs.

"Life with Refund Feature" Payout

For those who cannot tolerate the idea that the annuity they purchased might provide them with only a few income payments (because they could die soon after purchasing it) and then expire without value, a life-contingent annuity with a *"refund feature"* is often attractive. There are several varieties of refund features.

"Life and Period Certain"

The "Period Certain" refund feature of a life-contingent annuity payout comes into play only if the annuitant dies prior to the expiry of the refund feature "certain" period (e.g.: 10, 15, or 20 Years). For example, the most commonly used arrangement, "Life and 10 Year Certain", provides that the annuitant is guaranteed an income *for life* (which is why the feature is called "Life and.."), *and* that, if he or she dies prior to receiving 10 years' payments, the balance (10 years' payments, less the payments received by the annuitant) will be paid to the named beneficiary. As most life annuities are structured to provide *monthly* payments, this arrangement would guarantee at least 120 monthly payments (and is sometimes called "Life and 120 Months Certain").

This payout arrangement is often misunderstood, especially by older purchasers. The author recalls making a presentation of an immediate "Life and 10 Years Certain" annuity to an elderly woman whose response was "but what if I live longer than ten years?" She had heard his explanation that the annuity was for her lifetime, but was focused on the "10 Year" certain element. For this reason, the author has, for many years, recommended to insurance agents that they propose a more easily grasped refund feature – either "Cash Refund" or "Installment Refund"

"Life and Cash Refund"

The "Life and Cash Refund", like all life-contingent payout options, guarantees the annuitant an income for life, but provides that if the annuitant dies before the entire amount placed under annuitization - i.e.: the purchase price (for immediate annuities) or the annuitization value (for annuitized deferred annuities) – has not been paid out, the balance will be paid to the beneficiary in a single sum.

"Life and Installment Refund"

The "Life and Installment Refund" feature works like the "Life and Cash Refund" arrangement, except that the undistributed contract value will be paid to the beneficiary in installments. Either of these two methods is, in the author's opinion, far easier to understand than the "Life and Period Certain" method.

Joint Life Annuities ("Joint and Survivor")

A "Joint Life" or "Joint and Survivor" annuity payout arrangement (typically restricted to two annuitants) guarantees that annuity payments will persist for as long as *either* annuitant is living. The amount of the annuity payment may remain unchanged until the surviving annuitant dies ("Joint and 100% Survivor") or may be reduced at the death of the first annuitant (e.g.: "Joint and 2/3", in which the payment for the surviving annuitant will be 2/3 of the original amount).

A few insurers offer a "Joint and Survivor" payout with a refund feature, which guarantees benefits for the *longer of* the annuitants' lifetimes or the guarantee period.

The "Longevity Annuity"

The "longevity annuity" is a new type of annuity contract, arguably different from both the deferred and immediate types. Like an immediate life annuity, it provides only a guaranteed stream of income for life; there is no "accumulation value" that can be tapped prior to the Annuity Starting Date (ASD) – a future date – often, the attainment of a certain age (e.g.: age 85). The annuity benefit is guaranteed as to amount at the time of purchase. Some longevity annuities provide no benefit if the annuitant fails to live to the ASD; others provide a death benefit, payable to the named beneficiar(ies). Currently, relatively few insurers offer either type of contract.

The chief benefit of the longevity annuity is *financial leverage*. The benefit payment may be far larger than can be *guaranteed*, at the time of purchase, by any other instrument, including a deferred annuity. As one might expect, the leverage in a longevity annuity providing no benefit unless the annuitant lives to ASD is substantially greater than that provided by a contract with a death benefit.

Hypothetical Example: Joe, age 60, contributes $100,000 to a longevity annuity with no death benefit. If he survives to age 85, he will receive $110,000 each year for as long as he lives. A longevity annuity

Chapter 1: Annuity Basics

with a death benefit equal to his contribution, accumulated to the time of his death at 3% per year, will pay him a lifetime income, beginning at age 85, $75,000 per year.

The unpopularity of these contracts (few insurers offer them, and those that do have not experienced high sales volume) may be attributable to a fundamental misperception. The author, in discussing these contracts with insurance agents, has often heard "but that's a *terrible* investment!" And the author would agree – if the longevity were an "investment". But it's not. It's almost a pure *risk transfer* play. The purchaser who fears that his or her income will decline substantially or even cease as a result of adverse performance of his retirement income portfolio and/or excessive withdrawals from same may believe that *exchanging* a known sum of money today for the absolute assurance that he will have an income in his old age, in an amount greater than that which could be assured by alternatives, is an acceptable trade-off. The *risk* thus transferred is what actuaries call "superannuation" (living "too long" – i.e.: outliving one's financial resources).

For the financial advisor and the client, that client's purchase of a longevity annuity provides at least two significant benefits (apart from the possible benefit of a commission on the sale of that annuity).

First, it changes dramatically the nature of the "retirement income planning" problem. Planning for any client's retirement income involves two central quandaries: The first quandary is that no one can know what future returns on the client's retirement income portfolio will be. Even if one assumes such future returns (for purposes of projecting future portfolio value and the income it will produce), one cannot know *the order in which those assumed returns will occur* (often referred to as the "sequence of return risk"). The second quandary is that no one can know the duration over which retirement income must persist (because the client's date of death is unknowable). Thus, any retirement planning projection must *guess* as to (a) the annual returns of the client's portfolio, (b) the order in which assumed returns will occur, and (c) how long the client will live.

Including a longevity annuity in the client's overall retirement income planning amounts to installing a *defined benefit plan*. It amounts to converting the retirement income planning problem from one of indefinite duration to a "period certain" problem. If the annuity benefits are sufficient to ensure an acceptable lifestyle, the client's financial assets remaining (after purchase of the longevity annuity) need only provide income for a *known* period (from retirement to Annuity Starting Date).

The second benefit is that the client, having this "defined benefit plan" in place, and being thus assured that she will *never* "run out of income (or experience an income less than that guaranteed by the annuity), may be willing to engage in lifestyle activities that she would not otherwise consider, such as taking vacations, making gifts to heirs, etc. Indeed, in the author's opinion, this incentive for *behavioral change* may be the greatest advantage offered by a longevity annuity.

The "Contingent Annuity"

Recently, a number of Private Letter Rulings[4] have addressed an entirely new type of annuity – what some call a "contingent annuity". This is a contract, offered by an *issuer* (an insurance company, in the PLRs cited), to a *customer* holding an investment account at a sponsoring organization (the *sponsor*). The issuer guarantees that the customer/annuitant may make withdrawals from the investment not exceeding a specified percentage of a "benefit base" (which may be the greater of the account balance, the account balance at any prior anniversary date, or the account balance, accumulated at a given rate of interest) and, *if the account balance falls to zero* (as a result of adverse investment performance and/or subtractions from the account resulting from those withdrawals), the issuer will continue to make payments to the annuitant for his/her life (or the joint lifetime of the annuitant and spouse, if a "joint" option is elected).

Based on the PLRs cited, the benefits to the customer include –
- The assurance of an income for life not less than a specified percentage of the benefit base

11

- The advantage of "regular annuity rules" taxation of the income payments (i.e.: that a portion of each payment will be excludible from income as a *return of principal*)
- The advantage of "regular investment taxation" of the investment account – that is, that the investment account would *not* be considered "an annuity contract". Thus, while gains in the investment account would not enjoy the tax deferral of a deferred annuity contract, long term capital gain taxation would be available.

As of November, 2011, contingent annuities are not widely available. They have usually sold only through a very few Broker/Dealers and Registered Investment Advisory firms. Moreover, they are not approved for sales in some states. (New York has determined that a contingent annuity is a form of "financial guarantee insurance" and is therefore impermissible for sale in that state). However, several insurance companies have expressed interest in entering this market and have filed contingent annuity policy forms with some states that permit such offerings.

"Annuitization"

"Annuitization" refers to the conversion of *all or part of* the cash value of a deferred annuity to an income stream, the duration of which is determined by the payout option elected[5]. Prior to 2011, partial annuitization (annuitization of less than the entire contract value) was resisted by the IRS, which argued that it could not be achieved under existing Treasury regulations. The issue was resolved when Congress passed HR 5297, the Small Business Jobs Act of 2010. Section 2113 of that Act specifically provided that partial annuitization of deferred annuity contracts would be permissible. The tax treatment of this transaction will be discussed in Chapter 1.

Withdrawals

Annuitization is not the only way in which the owner of a deferred annuity may access contract values. Typically, these contracts allow for *partial withdrawals*. Withdrawals in excess of specified amounts or percentages of contract value during the surrender charge period are generally subject to surrender charges. Some contracts do not permit withdrawals during the first contract year. Most permit surrender charge free ("free") withdrawals of up to 10% of the contract value. Some contracts permit withdrawal of all previously credited interest. "Free" withdrawals may be limited to one per year.

Surrender Charges

Surrender charges are perhaps the most controversial elements of deferred annuities (immediate annuities generally have no surrender charges, as they usually cannot be surrendered for a lump sum). Some variable deferred annuities impose no surrender charges; these are generally designed to be sold by "fee only" advisors (who will be compensated by a management fee, rather than by a sales commission). Most variable deferred annuities and nearly all fixed deferred annuities do impose such charges.

Even an annuity that pays no sales commission costs money to put on the books; if the contract does not remain in force for long enough for the insurer to recoup (through investment earnings on the premium), the insurer will lose money. If a sales commission had been paid, it would lose even more. The purpose of surrender charges is to offset this potential loss. Because this loss can be recouped over time, surrender charges typically decline over time. A schedule for a deferred annuity that offers no up-front interest "bonus" might be 7,6,5,4,3,2,1,0 (7% of the contract's cash value if surrendered in the first year, 6% if surrendered in the second, etc., until the 8th year, when no surrender charge will be assessed).

Surrender charge schedules can vary considerably, from the relatively modest schedule described above to one that is both lengthy and substantial. One contract the author reviewed imposed charges for 15 years, grading down from a first year charge of 19.5% to zero in the 16th year. Surrender charges tend to increase as the selling commission increases and may be higher if a premium bonus in involved.

Surrender charges are sometimes perceived to be "owner detriments" – disadvantages to buying a deferred annuity - but this is an oversimplification. To be sure, for the consumer who requires access to the annuity cash value during the surrender period, these charges are a detriment, as they subject him or her to *liquidity risk*. But we should ask what *benefits* the annuity would be able to offer absent those charges. Few insurers would be willing to guarantee and/or guarantee the most competitive interest crediting and/or annuity payout rates without some assurance that the annuity will remain in force long enough to be profitable[6]. This is why many "low load" variable annuities imposing no surrender charges offer fewer *insurance* guarantees and, often, charge higher annual expenses than contracts with such charges.

Anyone offering advice regarding an annuity contract should be aware of its surrender charges and of when they do and do not apply. Regrettably, some contracts do not make this easy. Too often, the use of several different terms to describe contract value (see "What's This Annuity Worth?" below) can obscure how and when these charges are imposed.

"Bonus" Annuities

Some deferred annuities (both fixed and variable) offer "bonus" interest. Typically, this interest is added to the initial purchase amount (or, in the case of some contracts that accept recurring contributions, to all purchase payments made in the first few months or first contract year). The extent to which this "bonus" interest is *vested* varies. Some contracts vest it immediately; others vest it ratably over the surrender charge period. "Bonus" annuities typically impose longer and steeper surrender charge schedules than comparable contracts without a bonus.

"Tiered" Annuities

Some annuities encourage annuitization by crediting a "regular" interest rate to the contract's cash value and a higher rate to a second contract value that is used for annuitization purposes but is not available otherwise. Others seek almost to force annuitization by using a surrender charge schedule that never expires unless the owner annuitizes the contract over at least a minimum period of years.

A few contracts go even further - employing a surrender charge that not only never expires for the owner, but will apply to death proceeds, unless the beneficiary annuitizes over at least a minimum period of years. The reader may be surprised to learn that these contracts sell very well; in fact, the best selling index annuity in the U.S. was, for years, a contract of this type.

Why? For several reasons. It offered a strong "bonus" interest rate and a very competitive index-linked interest crediting formula. It also paid a very high commission. It could do so because the insurer knew that it was very likely to retain the use of the contract values for many years (because cashing it in would result in significant charges).

Market Value Adjustments

Some deferred annuities incorporate a "market value adjustment" (MVA) into their calculation of contract surrender value. The purpose of the MVA is to share with the policy owner the risk to the insurer that bond prices will be lower at the time of policy surrender than at the time of purchase. In that situation, the insurer will have to cash in more bonds to pay the annuity's surrender value than it would have, had bond prices not declined. As bond prices generally move adversely to interest rates, a bond with a 4.5% coupon rate, purchased by the insurer at par, will be worth less than its face amount if, five years later, interest rates have risen above 4.5% (because a buyer will not be willing to pay the face amount for an instrument paying less than the prevailing interest rate).

The MVA does not always work against the annuity owner because it is a *risk sharing* device. If interest rates *decline,* that same 4.5% bond will be paying *more* than the prevailing rate of interest; accordingly, its market value will be greater than par, as investors will be willing to pay for the income stream it provides. As it will be worth more to the insurer holding it, that insurer can credit a *positive*

MVA adjustment to the surrendered annuity backed by that bond (i.e.: an *increase* in the surrender value). Not all deferred annuities include this feature (which is not approved in some states).

Guaranteed Death Benefit Riders

Many variable and indexed deferred annuities offer the purchaser an optional "enhanced" death benefit that may exceed the contract's cash value. A typical rider would guarantee that the death benefit will be the greatest of

- the contract value at death

- the amount invested, compounded at a specified rate for a specified number of years or until a given age

- the contract value as of any prior policy anniversary

There are many variations, in both the cost and benefit, of this rider. One essential element, however, is that the death benefit it provides is not "life insurance"; it is an "amount not received as an annuity" and taxable as ordinary income, to the extent that it exceeds the owner's "investment in the contract".

"Guaranteed Living Benefit" Riders

A *very* popular feature of variable and indexed deferred annuities is the "guaranteed living benefit". There are four basic types:

1. The *Guaranteed Minimum Income Benefit (GMIB)*. This rider guarantees a minimum income *for life* – calculated as a percentage of the rider's "benefit base" - regardless of policy performance. To the author's knowledge, no fixed annuities offer this rider (which makes sense, as those annuities provide guarantees of principal and minimum interest); it is still offered by many variable annuities, but is much less popular today than the Guaranteed Lifetime

Withdrawal Benefit (GMIB) described below.

The *benefit base* of the GMIB is typically the buyer's investment, increased by additions of a guaranteed "GMIB interest rate" until annuitization under the rider is elected. Typically, if the contract value exceeds the benefit base at any point where a "step up" option is available, the owner may elect to increase the benefit base to that [greater] contract value; the benefit base will, in that event, continue to be credited with the GMIB interest.

The GMIB requires *annuitization,* and the annuitization decision is generally irrevocable. Moreover, annuitization using the GMIB "benefit base" generally uses special annuity payout factors less favorable than those used for normal contract annuitization. An "age setback" may also be required (e.g.: Joan, age 65, wishes to annuitize the GMIB "benefit base" of her annuity; her contract uses a 6 year age setback, so the amount she will receive from the GMIB each year will be determined by application of the special GMIB payout factors for a female age 59).

These restrictions - the low annuity payout factors, age setback, and the requirement that the contract be annuitized – make the GMIB look unattractive to many consumers, which is why it is seldom sold these days. But it can offer advantages over a withdrawal benefit (e.g.: GMIB guaranteed interest crediting to the benefit base may continue while the owner takes withdrawals; typically, a guaranteed *withdrawal* benefit guarantees interest crediting on the benefit base only until the first withdrawal).

It is absolutely *essential* that the buyer of an annuity with a GMIB understand that this rider guarantees only an *income; it does not guarantee a future lump sum.* Moreover, the guaranteed interest rate credited to the benefit base is *not*

Chapter 1: Annuity Basics

a "return on investment", as it can be received only in the form of GMIB annuity payments.

2. The *Guaranteed Minimum Accumulation Benefit (GMAB)* does guarantee a future lump sum. Typically, it guarantees the original principal, perhaps increased by a guaranteed interest rate, after a waiting period, regardless of contract performance. Life the GMIB, the GMAB has declined in popularity in recent years.

3. The *Guaranteed Minimum Withdrawal Benefit (GMWB)* guarantees a minimum income, regardless of policy performance and does not require the contract to be annuitized. Like the GMIB, the GMWB guarantees an income from a *benefit base* (the chief difference being that the GMIB requires annuitization of that benefit base, while the GMWB merely amortizes it over a period of years). A 7% GMWB would guarantee that, no matter how the annuity policy performs, the owner may elect to make withdrawals of up to 7% of the benefit base, and that withdrawals of that same amount will persist for 14.3 years (100% of benefit base, divided by 7% annual withdrawals, equals 14.3 years). Like the GMIB, the GMWB often includes a "step up" feature, providing that, if the annuity cash value exceeds the GMWB benefit base at any point where a "step up" option is exercisable, the benefit base will be increased to that greater value.

4. The *Guaranteed Lifetime Withdrawal Benefit (GLWB)* is viewed by some as a form of the GMWB. That is true – and when the GLWB is described as a "GMWB *for life*", the distinction is clear. But to avoid confusion, this author prefers to use the term GMWB to describe a withdrawal benefit that guarantees withdrawals of a certain amount *for as long as the benefit base lasts* and GLWB to describe the rider that guarantees that such withdrawals will continue, unreduced (but possibly increased, by application of a "step up" of the benefit

base) for the life of the owner (or joint lifetime of the owner and spouse, if that option was elected)[7].

The Guarantee Lifetime Withdrawal Benefit, like all guaranteed living benefits, is an *insurance* feature. It transfers a specified risk (that the income produced by the annuity contract will decline, due to poor performance) from the purchaser to the annuity issuer. Regrettably, however, this rider is often analyzed purely as an *investment* feature; its cost is, in many studies, measured against its expected benefit with the object of determining if it will "pay off". Thus, some studies have focused on the probability that a consumer owning a GLWB and electing lifetime withdrawals will ever receive other than "his own money" (i.e.: the cash value of the annuity). This rationale is fatally flawed because it treats the GLWB as *an investment* that should be profitable for any purchaser; it fails to recognize that the GLWB is *insurance,* and that *no* insurance policy, of *any* kind, is designed to "pay off" *on average.* If that were not so, insurers would never make a profit.

Chapter 1: Annuity Basics

1 *Tax Facts on Insurance and Employee Benefits* [hereafter, "*Tax Facts*"] 2011, Vol. 2, (National Underwriter Co.), Q.3501

2 *Ibid;* Treas. Reg. §1.72-2(b)

3 A *very few* immediate annuities provide that annuity payments will increase with reference to an internal index such as the Consumer Price Index. Most require the purchaser to select the annual increase percentage at purchase.

4 PLRs 200949007, 201002016, 201129029

5 Strictly speaking, "annuitization" might be considered to apply to immediate annuities as well, but the term is generally used in connection with deferred annuities.

6 While it is true that deferred annuities issued currently generally offer higher interest rates to contracts having multi-year interest rate guarantees and surrender charge schedules than to contracts with short term guarantees (and surrender charge schedules), this has not always been the case. This may be due to the nature of the "interest rate curve" at the time of policy issue and/or to the fact that multi-year guarantees require greater policy reserves.

7 Some authors, including the authors of some excellent studies on the value of the GLWB, persist in referring to that rider as a GMWB. In view of the fact that, as of this writing (July, 2011), many issuers of variable annuities offer *both* a withdrawal benefit with a lifetime guarantee (GLWB) *and* one that guarantees only the return of the benefit base (GMWB), this author suggests that the distinction in benefit duration be reflected in the name by which we call the feature. Guaranteed Minimum Withdrawal Benefit (GMWB) and Guaranteed Lifetime Withdrawal Benefit (GLWB) works well, and many insurers call their offering by those labels. At the very least, those who insist upon referring to lifetime benefit provisions as "GMWB" should add "for life" to that label.

Chapter Two: Taxation of Annuities During Lifetime

The rules governing taxation of annuities are contained in Internal Revenue Code section 72 ("the Code") and the applicable Treasury Regulations. While this section deals with both annuities purchased inside IRAs and qualified plans, we will be concerned, in this book, chiefly with the rules applying to so-called "non-qualified" annuities (annuities purchased with after-tax dollars outside of such plans). For example, we will address the tax rules regarding the deferral of tax on annual earnings within annuities and with the methods for determining how much of each regular annuity payment is taxable, which rules refer only to non-qualified annuity contracts.

"Qualified" annuities are governed by those parts of the Code dealing with the specific type of plan the annuity is funding (e.g.: Section 408 for traditional IRAs, Section 408A for Roth IRAs, and Section 401 for pension plans). *The rules that govern taxation of an annuity purchased to fund an IRA or qualified plan are totally inapplicable to an annuity purchased outside such plans.* A common mistake made by advisors in the area of retirement planning is to apply "regular annuity rules" (pertaining to a non-qualified annuity to an annuity inside an IRA or qualified plan.

> The rules that would govern an annuity purchased to fund an IRA or qualified plan are totally inapplicable to an annuity purchased outside of such plans

While the taxation of non-qualified annuities can be very complex, there are two very simple rules that one must bear in mind:
1. *All* distributions from *any* annuity, to the extent that they are taxable, will be taxable as *ordinary income.* *No* annuity contract *ever* receives capital gains treatment (under current law).
2. *All* distributions from *any* annuity are taxed in one of two ways: *"Amounts received as an annuity"* or *"amounts not received as an annuity".*

> All distributions from a non-qualified annuity, whether made to a living contract owner or to a beneficiary, are taxed as either (a) "*amounts received as an annuity*" or (b) "*amounts not received as an annuity*"

"Amounts received as an annuity"

While the term "annuity" can be used to describe a commercial annuity *contract*, "amounts received as an annuity" generally refers only to the income stream produced by *an immediate annuity* or *a deferred annuity that has been annuitized* (that is: placed under a regular annuity payout option).

Treasury Regulation 1.72-2(b)(2) defines "amounts not received as an annuity as *only* those payments that meet the following tests:

(i) They must be received on or after the "annuity starting date" as that term is defined in paragraph (b) of §1.72–4;

(ii) They must be payable in periodic installments at regular intervals (whether annually, semiannually, quarterly, monthly, weekly, or otherwise) over a period of more than one full year from the annuity starting date; and

(iii) Except as indicated in subparagraph (3) of this paragraph, the total of the amounts payable must be determinable at the annuity starting date either directly from the terms of the contract or indirectly by the use of either mortality tables or compound interest computations, or both, in conjunction with such terms and in accordance with sound actuarial theory.

These payments are taxed under the "regular annuity rules" of IRC Sect. 72(b), in which a portion of each annuity payment is excluded from tax, by use of an "exclusion ratio", as a *return of principal*, and the remainder (that represents contract "gain") is taxed as ordinary income[1]. For contracts with an annuity starting date prior to January 1, 1987, the exclusion ratio continues to apply, even after all the principal has been recovered. Partial withdrawals are not *generally* considered "amounts received as an annuity". However, some "guaranteed withdrawal benefits" have been held, by the IRS, to qualify as "amounts received as an annuity"[2]. A recent (March, 2011) Private Letter Ruling held that a "contingent annuity" (an investment contract that obligated a corporation to pay a benefit to an investment account if the account value falls below a specified amount) will be treated as an annuity contract under §72 and that "the benefit payments made pursuant thereto will be considered "amounts received as an annuity" [3]

For *fixed* annuities, the exclusion ratio is *total investment in the contract* divided by the *expected return*. For a "Period Certain" annuity, the expected return is the sum of the guaranteed payments. For a "life-contingent" annuity, the expected return is the annual annuity payment multiplied by the life expectancy of the annuitant, using IRS annuity tables (see *Tax Facts*, 2011, Q. 3509). If the annuity includes a "refund feature", the *investment in the contract* must be adjusted by the value of that feature (see *Tax Facts*, 2011, Q. 3511).

For a *variable* annuity, the expected return is not known; thus, the excludible portion is determined by dividing the *investment in the contract* (adjusted for the cost of the refund element guarantee) by the number of years over which payments are expected to persist, using the IRS annuity tables (see *Tax Facts*, 2011, Q. 3522).

"Amounts not received an an annuity"

All other distributions from a deferred annuity (including "deemed distributions") – whether made during the lifetime of the owner or annuitant – or made after owner or annuitant's death - are "amounts not received as an annuity". These include –
- Partial withdrawals
- Partial or total policy surrenders (except where surrender is made pursuant to a tax free exchange under IRC §1035)
- Loans taken against the annuity contract

- Cash value of the contract to the extent that it is pledged as collateral for a loan made to the owner by a third-party lender
- Gift or sale of the contract

The tax treatment of "amounts not received as an annuity" will depend upon the date of issue of the contract.

"Amounts Not Received As An Annuity" From Contracts Entered Into Before August 14, 1982

Non-annuity distributions from contracts entered into before August 14, 1982 *and allocated to investments made before that date* are taxed using the "principal first" rule. All such distributions are deemed to be non-taxable returns of principal until all principal has been distributed[4]. This treatment is accorded to any contract issued after August 13, 1982 if acquired via a tax-free exchange (under IRC §1035) from a contract issued prior to that date (but only with respect to distributions allocated to investments made prior to August 14, 1982).

"Amounts Not Received As An Annuity" From Contracts Entered Into After August 13, 1982

For contracts entered into after August 13, 1982, "amounts not received as an annuity" will be taxed according to the "interest first" rule. All such distributions will be taxed as Ordinary Income until all "gain" in the contract has been distributed.

Tax Deferral of Gain in a Deferred Annuity

One of the advantages of a deferred annuity is that annual increases in contract value ("gain") are not generally subject to income tax until distributed. There is no section of the Internal Revenue Code which specifically grants this treatment; it is granted *by implication*. As the annual growth in the annuity is neither "an amount received as an annuity" nor "an amount not received as an annuity", the crediting of such growth is not a taxable event.

Annuities Held by Non-Natural Persons

Such tax deferral does not, however, apply to all deferred annuities. Section 72(u) of the Code states that if any annuity contract is held by "a person who is not a natural person", the contract will not be treated as an annuity for income tax law purposes and the income on the contract for any taxable year will be treated as ordinary income received or accrued by the contract owner during such taxable year. "A person who is not a natural person" refers to entities other than human beings – e.g.: corporations, trusts, etc.

This rule applies to all annuities held by such non-natural persons, *with respect to contributions made after February 28, 1986*[5], unless one or more of five exceptions applies. The exceptions, listed items A through E of §72(u)(3) are any annuity which –
 (A) is acquired by the estate of a decedent by reason of the death of the decedent,
 (B) is held under a plan described in section 401 (a) or 403 (a), under a program described in section 403 (b), or under an individual retirement plan,
 (C) is a qualified funding asset (as defined in section 130 (d), but without regard to whether there is a qualified assignment),
 (D) is purchased by an employer upon the termination of a plan described in section 401 (a) or 403 (a) and is held by the employer until all amounts under such contract are distributed to the employee for whom such contract was purchased or the employee's beneficiary, or
 (E) is an immediate annuity.

However, §72(u)(1) supplies an additional "safe harbor", stating that "for purposes of this paragraph, holding by a trust or other entity as an agent for a natural person shall not be taken into account".

The IRS has held, in Private Letter Rulings[6], that trusts, both revocable and irrevocable, may qualify as such. However, in all rulings of which the author is aware, the trusts had no beneficiaries which were not "natural persons". Therefore, it is questionable whether any deferred annuity held by an irrevocable trust the beneficiaries of which include at least one "non-natural person" would qualify for the §72(u)(1) exception, and, thus, enjoy tax deferral of gain. The taxation of annuities held by and/or payable to a Trust will be discussed in more detail in Chapter 3 (Annuities and Trusts).

What about annuities owned by corporations? While the legislative history of §72(u) shows that Congress intended to deny tax-deferral, in general, to corporate-owned annuities, the Service has acknowledged that, in certain cases, such contracts will be treated as "annuities"[7]. With respect to ownership of an annuity by a pass-through entity such as a Family Limited Partnership or Family Limited Liability Company, there is no clear authority. However, as Gary Underwood observes, "since these business entities generally have an independent business purpose and do not simply hold legal title like a trust, they arguably are not agents or nominal owners for the entity owners. Although each of these entities usually has flow-through income tax treatment, each nevertheless could access policy values to meet its business or creditor obligations"[8]. In responding to a request for a Private Letter Ruling (even though the taxpayer withdrew the request, the Service held that *Under the present facts, Partnership is not a mere agent holding the deferred annuities for natural persons, rather it is proposed that Partnership actually receive and possess the deferred annuities as property of Partnership, thus, subjecting this property to any possible claims of creditors against Partnership. By way of contrast, the example set forth in the drafting history of §72(u) clearly demonstrates that the agency exception was limited to a situation where a pure agency was created as the nonnatural person holding the property had no interest other than as agent.*"[9]

Partial vs. Full Surrenders

While the gain in a non-annuity distribution will always be taxed as Ordinary Income, the amount of gain in such distribution will depend upon whether it is a total surrender or a partial withdrawal. In the event of a partial surrender (i.e., a withdrawal for any amount les than the full value of the contract), the amount of gain is determined as the excess of the contract value over the investment in the contract (cost basis), *without regard to any surrender charges*. Thus, the amount of gain is calculated based on the *gross* cash value of the annuity, to determine whether any of a withdrawal will be attributable to gain and subject to income taxation.[10]

On the other hand, if the withdrawal represents a full surrender of the contract, the normal rule for withdrawals just stated does not apply.[11] The tax code explicitly indicates that, for full surrenders, the amount of gain shall be the excess of the amount received (i.e., the actual net surrender value received) over the investment in the contract (cost basis).[12]

Example: Taxpayer holds an annuity that was purchased for $100,000 (the investment in the contract). The current cash value of the annuity is $105,000, and the annuity has a $10,000 surrender charge. Thus, the net surrender value of the annuity would be $95,000. If the taxpayer takes a partial withdrawal, the amount of gain in the contract would be $5,000, based on the current cash value of $105,000, without regard to any surrender charges. Thus, any partial withdrawal will be taxable up to the first $5,000 of gain, and any excess will be treated as a return of principal. However, if the entire annuity is surrendered, the total amount received will be $95,000. As the investment in the contract is $100,000, the taxpayer will report no gain[13], and will be eligible for a $5,000 loss.

Reducing the Tax on Partial Withdrawals through Multiple Contracts

As we have seen, for contracts issued after August 13, 1982, withdrawals are taxable up to the amount of "gain" in the contract. One way to reduce the impact of this "interest first" treatment is to use multiple contracts.

Example: John purchases a single deferred annuity contract for $100,000 which, five years later, has a cash value of $120,000. If John then withdraws $15,000, the entire amount withdrawn will be taxable as Ordinary Income (and may be subject to the early distribution penalty tax of 10% if no exception applies).

Had John purchased ten deferred annuity contracts, each for $10,000 which, five years later, have cash values of $12,000 each ($120,000 total), and he *surrenders one for its full value ($12,000) and takes a partial withdrawal of $3,000 from a second (for a total distribution of $15,000), his tax would be only $4,000 (the gain in both contracts). Moreover, if the early distribution penalty applies, that penalty will be only $400 (10% of $4,000), rather than $1,500 (10% of $15,000).*

Congress recognized this technique as abusive and enacted IRC §72(e)(12), which treats all annuities issued during a single calendar year and issued by the same insurance company as one annuity, for purposes of taxing withdrawals. This provision does not apply either to partial withdrawals or to surrender of deferred annuity contracts issued in the same calendar year by different insurance companies.

Deductibility of a Loss in a Deferred Annuity

An income tax deduction for a loss may be taken by a taxpayer only when the loss is incurred in connection with the taxpayer's trade or business or in a transaction entered into for profit.[14]

Generally, an annuity contract is considered to have been purchased for profit, and thus, "if a taxpayer sustains a loss upon surrender of a refund annuity contract, he may claim a deduction for the loss, regardless of whether he purchased the contract in connection with his trade or business or as a personal investment"[15]. The loss is an ordinary one, not a capital loss[16].

How is this loss claimed on taxpayer's income tax return? While some suggest otherwise, there is general agreement that the loss should be taken as a miscellaneous itemized deduction subject to the 2% floor, in light of IRC section 67(b) which states that all deductions are miscellaneous itemized deductions unless specifically listed in §67(b)(1) through §67(b)(12) – and deferred annuities surrendered at a loss are not so enumerated.

Penalty for Early Distributions from an Annuity

Deferred annuities are long-term instruments, designed to produce a dependable income for the buyer's retirement. In granting the benefit of tax-deferral to these instruments, Congress imposed restrictions to discourage their use as short-term savings vehicles by enacting IRC section 72(q), which imposes a 10% penalty tax on certain "premature" payments (distributions) from annuity contracts. This penalty applies only to payments to the extent that they are includible in taxable income and does not apply at all to certain distributions. Distributions excluded from the penalty, under IRC §72(q)(2) are those –

(A) made on or after the date on which the taxpayer attains age 59½;

(B) made on or after the death of the holder (or, where the holder is not an individual, the death of the primary annuitant);

(C) attributable to the taxpayer becoming disabled;

(D) which are a part of a series of substantially equal periodic payments (not less frequently than annually) made for the life (or life expectancy) of the taxpayer or the joint lives (or joint life expectancies) of the taxpayer and his designated beneficiary;

(E) from a qualified pension, profit sharing, or stock bonus plan, §403(b) annuity plan, or IRA;

(F) allocable to investment in the contract before August 14, 1982;

(G) under a qualified funding asset;

(H) subject to the 10% penalty for withdrawals from a qualified retirement plan;

(I) under an immediate annuity contract;

(J) which are purchased by an employer upon the termination of a qualified plan and which is held by the employer until such time as the employee separates from service.

The exemption for an immediate annuity is not absolute. Revenue Ruling 92-95 states that "where a deferred annuity contract was *exchanged* (emphasis added) for an immediate annuity contract, the purchase date of the new contract for purposes of the 10% penalty tax was considered to be the date upon which the deferred annuity was purchased. Thus, payments from the replacement contract did not fall within the immediate annuity exception to the penalty tax."[17]

Where an immediate annuity is purchased directly, its payments will always be penalty-free; If, however, it is acquired as part of an exchange from a deferred annuity contract, it will not escape the §72(q) penalty unless the payments happen to meet another exception.

Example. George, age 45, purchases a 5 Year "Period Certain" Single Premium Immediate Annuity (SPIA). Payments under that contract will escape the penalty because they qualify for the immediate annuity exception of §72(q)(2)(I).

Harry (also under age 59 ½) owns a deferred annuity with substantial "gain" and wishes to take the proceeds over five years. He attempts to avoid the penalty on that gain (which would apply if he were to annuitize his contract over a period less than his life expectancy) by exchanging his deferred annuity for an identical 5 Year "Period Certain" SPIA. Harry's income payments will be subject to the penalty because the purchase date of the original contract is more than one year earlier than annuity starting date of the new contract (*IRC §72(u)(4)(B) and Revenue Ruling 92-95*).

Had Harry's new annuity been payable for his lifetime, he would have avoided the penalty, because the exception of §72(q)(2)(D) would apply (as it would have if Harry had annuitized the original contract on a "life annuity" basis).

72(q)(2) Exceptions where the annuity is held by a trust

Where an annuity is held by a grantor trust, the applicability of the §72(q)(2) exceptions is unclear. With regard to the age 59

½ exception, the IRS has confirmed in a 2001 General Information Letter that the measuring life will be that of the grantor[18]. It is not clear from that Letter, however, whether the exceptions for disability might be satisfied by the grantor's disability or whether the Substantially Equal Periodic Payments exception could be claimed for payments made over grantor's lifetime.

As to the exception of distributions made upon death of the holder of an annuity it is not entirely clear whether the death of a grantor of a trust will trigger that exception if the annuitant is other than the grantor. §72(q)(2)(B) states that it applies to distributions "made on or after the death of the holder **(or, where the holder is not an individual, the death of the primary annuitant)** [emphasis added]. That language is clear. Where a non-natural person (such as a trust) owns a deferred annuity, the primary annuitant is deemed to be the "holder" (owner). This same deemed designation occurs in §72(s), which governs required distributions from an annuity upon holder's death. §72(s)(6)(A) states "For purposes of this subsection, if the holder of the contract is not an individual, the primary annuitant shall be treated as the holder of the contract". It should be noted, however, that the subsection referred to, in that sentence, is §72(s), not §72(q).

What makes the issue unclear is the extent to which (if at all) the grantor trust rules of §671-677 "trump" the clear language of §72(q)(2)(B). J. Gary Underwood acknowledges that

> "Alternatively, one might argue that the death of a nongrantor annuitant triggers the death distribution rules, even for grantor trusts. Although no authority explicitly addresses this issue, distribution at the death of the grantor is the most logical choice. Since the grantor is the owner of grantor trust assets for income tax purposes, and the death of the owner is the primary trigger for annuity distributions at death, then the death of the grantor should trigger the death distribution requirements. It seems incorrect to assert that the

grantor is the owner of the annuity for income tax purposes, but the grantor is not the owner for the income tax requirement of distributions at death under IRC Sec. 72. Although some insurance companies treat the death of the grantor as a distribution event, it is possible that other insurance companies may not be aware of the death of a nonannuitant grantor and may not have reporting procedures in place to trigger a distribution"[19].

The implications of the grantor trust rules for trust-owned annuities are profound and, regrettably, not entirely clear. Is the gift of a deferred annuity by a grantor to his/her grantor trust an income taxable event? The answer may depend upon whom you ask. We will examine that question in Chapter 4 (Annuities and Trusts).

In the case of an annuity held by a non-grantor trust, where the trust taxpayer has no age or life expectancy, it seems clear that the trust would be ineligible to claim the premature withdrawal exception on account on age 59 ½, disability, or for substantially equal periodic payments. Of course, where the trust is not able to claim the "agent of a natural person" exemption of §72(u)(1), the annuity will not be treated as an annuity for tax purposes – making all gains in the contract taxable annually. In that scenario, the 72(q) penalty will be moot, except with respect to the current year's gain.

Exchanges of an annuity

IRC §1035 provides that no gain or loss shall be recognized on the exchange of a life insurance policy for an annuity or an annuity for another annuity. (The exchange of an annuity for a life insurance policy *does not* qualify under §1035). The acquired annuity receives the basis of the transferred contract, under the "like-kind exchanged" rules.

Where the annuity or life insurance policy is exchanged, not solely in kind, but, rather in exchange for another policy or annuity of lesser value, and where transferor receives cash or other property as part of the exchange, that excess is "boot", with the result that transferor must recognize, in the year of exchange, the lesser of the unrecognized gain in the transferred contract or the boot received.[20] However, if the exchange of an annuity meeting the requirements of §1935 results in a loss, no loss will recognized, regardless of whether the exchange involves the receipt of boot.[21] The application of §1035 to an exchange is automatic, provided its provisions are met; it is not an election.

Partial Exchanges of an Annuity

For years, the IRS fought *partial* tax free exchanges of annuity contracts as tax-avoidance schemes. However, in *Conway v. Commissioner*[22], the Tax Court held that the direct exchange by an insurance company of a portion of an existing annuity contract to an unrelated insurance company for a new annuity contact was a tax-free exchange under §1035. In **Revenue Ruling 2003-76**, the IRS provided guidance on tax-free exchanges of annuities. In that case, the taxpayer transferred a portion of the surrender value of an existing deferred annuity to a new annuity issued by a different insurer. The ruling concluded that the transaction was a tax-free exchange under §1035 and that the basis and investment in the contract was to be allocated ratably between the contracts, based upon the amount of cash value transferred. The IRS acquiesced in the Tax Court's opinion in *Conway*, and provided guidance in Rev. Ruling 2003-76. In that ruling, the taxpayer had assigned 60% of the cash value of a deferred annuity to a new insurer, to be deposited into a new deferred annuity contract. The IRS ruled that after the exchange, taxpayer's adjusted basis in the new contract would be 60% of the adjusted basis in the original contract immediately prior to the exchange and that the basis in the original contract would be 40% of its basis prior to the exchange. The taxpayer's "investment in the contract" would, the IRS ruled, be similarly adjusted.

The Service provided further guidance on "partial 1035 exchanges" of annuities in **Rev. Proc. 2008-24**. In that revenue procedure, a partial transfer of cash value from one annuity to a new contract will qualify under §1035 if certain requirements are met:

1. No amount will be withdrawn from, or received in surrender of, either contract for 12 months beginning on the date of transfer *or if*
2. transferor/taxpayer demonstrates that one of the conditions described in §72(q)(2)(A), (B), (C), (E) (F), (G), (H), or (J) or any similar life event "occurred between" the date of transfer and the date of the withdrawal or surrender.

In June, 2011, the Treasury clarified some of the uncertainties arising from the language of Rev. Proc. 2008-34 by releasing **Rev. Proc. 2011-38.** While it resolved some uncertainties (especially, with regard to when the occurrence of the "safe harbor" events of death, disability, etc. of the cited paragraphs of §72(q)(2) would have to occur for the partial exchange to be valid if withdrawals occur within a waiting period after the transfer) and while it reduces the duration of that waiting period by half, the rules of this Revenue Procedure are actually more restrictive than the earlier one. It provides that a partial transfer of cash value from an existing deferred annuity to a new one will qualify under §1035 if no amounts are withdrawn from, or received by surrender of, either annuity contract during the **180 days** beginning on the date of the transfer. But it eliminates the "safe harbors" of the earlier procedure (that is, if the death, disability, or other qualifying event described in §72(q)(2)(A), (B), (C), (E), (F), (G), (H), or (J) "occurred between" the date of transfer and the date of the withdrawal). Now, a withdrawal within 180 days of the transfer will cause the exchange to fail under §1035, regardless of whether any of those events occurred during that period. This Rev. Proc. will apply to covered transfers made on or after October 24th, 2011. Transfers made prior to that date will be subject to the rules of Rev. Proc. 2008-24.

Transfer of an Annuity by Sale or Gift

The transfer of an annuity from an owner to another taxpayer may have both *income tax* and *gift tax* consequences.

Gift of a Deferred Annuity

While gifts are not generally subject to income tax (because gifts are not "income"), the gift of an annuity may have *gift tax* consequences to the transferor **and** *income tax* consequences, either to the transferor, transferee, or both. The income tax consequences depend upon when the annuity was issued.

The transfer of an Annuity *issued after April 22, 1987* is treated as if the donor received, on the date of transfer, the "gain" in the contract (the cash surrender value of the contract, less donor's "investment in the contract") as "an amount not received as an annuity"[23]. Donee's cost basis will be donor's adjusted basis, plus donee's cost (if any), increased by any *gift tax* actually paid. The transfer will also be subject to *gift tax*.

If the annuity had been issued prior to April 23, 1987, the results are more complicated. The income tax consequences will be triggered, not at the time of the gift, but only when the annuity is surrendered by the donee. Upon such surrender, donor will recognize ordinary income to the extent of the gain in the contract *as of the date of the gift*. Any gain accruing from the date of the gift to the date of surrender will be reported as income by the donee.

Not all gratuitous transfers of annuities produce these results. These rules do not apply to transfers between spouses or to former spouses incident to a divorce. Moreover, the IRS has ruled that the transfer of an annuity from a trust to a trust beneficiary for less than full and adequate consideration was not a taxable event[24].

Sale of an annuity

The transfer of an annuity (which includes an owner's naming a new owner) in exchange for full and adequate consideration is a sale of that annuity. The seller must recognize any gain in the contract as ordinary income[25].

When the annuity sold is in "payout status" (that is, had been annuitized[26], the seller's cost basis must be reduced – but not below zero - by the cumulative excludible portions of annuity payments received. (In other words, the taxable gain cannot exceed the sale price). Where an annuity contract is sold for *less than its cost basis,* it appears that the seller realizes an ordinary loss[27].

Transfer of an annuity to a trust

While the transfer of ownership of an annuity is, generally speaking, a taxable event for both gift and income tax purposes, the tax consequences of a transfer of an annuity to a trust depend upon the nature of the trust. Moreover, when the receiving trust is a grantor trust (with respect to the transferor), the *income tax* (but *not* the *gift tax*) consequences are not entirely clear.

Transfer (either by sale or gift) to transferor's *revocable* trust

The transfer of an annuity from an owner to the owner's revocable trust is not a taxable event for income or gift tax purposes because the property in a revocable trust remains under the "dominion and control" of the trustor and one cannot make a sale or gift to oneself.

Transfer, *by sale,* to transferor's *irrevocable grantor trust*

This transfer is generally acknowledged not to be a true "sale", under the well-established rule that a sale to one's own grantor trust (even an irrevocable one) is not a taxable event *for income tax purposes.*

Transfer, *by gift,* to transferor's *irrevocable grantor trust*

Many, if not most, authorities would probably assert that the same holds true when the transfer is *by gift* from A to A's irrevocable grantor trust, by application of the same rule. However, the *income tax* results of the transfer of an annuity *by gift* are subject to a very specific rule that does not comport with the grantor trust rules. IRC §72(e)(4)(C) states that "if an individual who holds an annuity contract transfers it without full and adequate consideration, such individual shall be treated as receiving an amount equal to the excess of the cash surrender value of such contract at the time of transfer over the investment in such contract at such time" and that the gain thus recognized shall be treated as "an amount not received as an annuity".

Clearly, there is an incompatibility between these two rules, both the product of Congressional legislation, and it is difficult (for this author, at least) to discern if Congress intended one to "trump" the other, or, indeed, if it recognized the incongruity. The same 99th Congress that enacted IRC §72(s)(6)(A) (which declares that, when an annuity is held by a non-natural person, the primary annuitant shall be deemed to be the holder) addressed and expanded the grantor trust rules by adding §672(e), which treats the settler as holding any power or interest held by settlor's spouse[28].

Similarly, in enacting §72(s), the 99th Congress provided some "parity" in the rules governing post-death distributions from non-qualified annuities and the rules governing post-death distributions from IRAs and qualified plans (§401(a)(9)). Both require a default payout period of five years (which, for IRAs and qualified plans, applies only if the plan participant/IRA holder dies prior to Required Beginning Date), and two allowable exceptions – annuitization over life expectancy (§72(s)(2) for annuities; §401(a)(9)(B)(iii) for IRAs and qualified plans) and "spousal continuation" (§72(s)(3) for annuities and §401(a)(9)(B)(iv) for IRAs and qualified plans).

Yet, in enacting the "annuitization, if payments begin within one year" requirement of §72(s)(2) for deferred annuities (part of that "parity"), Congress appears to have forgotten completely the existence of §72(h) which requires that annuitization by a beneficiary be elected within *sixty days* of death (or, more precisely, of "60 days after the day on which [the death benefit] first became payable").

What can one make of such incongruities in our tax law? Perhaps only that they exist and that, absent guidance from Treasury or the IRS as to how to resolve them, one should interpret the rules involved in way that makes the most sense - or, at the least, produces the most consistency.

Clearly, Congress intended that the transfer by gift of an annuity from one taxpayer to another will cause recognition of all gain by transferor in the year of transfer. The question remains as to whether such a transaction, between a taxpayer and a trust treated as a grantor trust with respect to that taxpayer, is covered by that rule. Did Congress envision this situation when it passed §72(e)(4)(C)? Should one assume that, in enacting that provision, Congress was fully aware of the grantor trust rules and that application of those rules would deem the transferor and transferee in this situation to be the same individual? Even if one is unsure of the answer to either question, does it "make sense" to apply the grantor trust rules to this transaction simply for the sake of consistency? Does it make sense to hold that A is the taxpayer with respect to A's grantor trust for all purposes save the gift of an annuity? Unless and until the Service provides guidance on this issue, the practitioner will have to use his or her own best judgment.

Transfer to transferor's *irrevocable, non-grantor* trust

This one's easy. §72(e)(4)(C) clearly applies.

Partial Annuitization

Until the passage of the Small Business Jobs Act of 2010, the tax treatment of income produced by the *partial* annuitization of a deferred annuity contract was uncertain. Would the income be taxed as "amounts received as an annuity" under the "exclusion rules" of IRC §72(b) or as *withdrawals* (that is: "amounts not received as an annuity")? While insurance industry advocates insisted that the former was a reasonable result, IRS officials had questioned whether partial annuitization was possible under existing IRS regulations.

Section 2113 of the Act (HR 5297) provides that

> "*If any amount is received as an annuity for a period of 10 years or more or during one or more lives under any portion of an annuity, endowment, or life insurance contract--*

'(A) such portion shall be treated as a separate contract for purposes of this section,

'(B) for purposes of applying subsections (b), (c), and (e), the investment in the contract shall be allocated pro rata between each portion of the contract from which amounts are received as an annuity and the portion of the contract from which amounts are not received as an annuity, and

'(C) a separate annuity starting date under subsection (c)(4) shall be determined with respect to each portion of the contract from which amounts are received as an annuity.'.

To qualify for treatment as "amounts received as an annuity" (and, thus, for the "exclusion ratio" treatment of IRC §72(b)), annuity payments must persist for at least ten years or for the lives of one or more annuitants. The taxpayer's *investment in the contract* will be allocated on a *pro rata* basis between the annuitized and non-annuitized portions of the contract. Moreover, a new *annuity starting date* will be determined for each portion.

Annuities Held In IRAs

As we have seen, the tax rules governing nonqualified annuities can be confusing. A further source of confusion is the extent to which those same rules apply to annuities held within IRAs. Quite simply, they do not. An annuity held within an IRA simply an IRA asset, and, with only two exceptions, is treated like any other plan asset. The exceptions are (a) determination of Required Minimum Distribution of an annuity held in a Traditional IRA and (b) determination of the fair market value of a deferred annuity held in a Traditional IRA for purposes of a "Roth conversion".

Required Minimum Distribution for an Annuity Held In A Traditional IRA

When an annuity, either in payout status or not in payout status, is held in an IRA, the Required Minimum Distribution rules applying to that annuity are modified as follows:

If the annuity is in payout status over the lifetime of the annuitant (or the lifetimes of the annuitant and a beneficiary), the annuity payments will be considered to satisfy the RMD rules of §401(a)(9)[29]. In other words, there is no need to calculate the RMD using the normal method. In fact, that method would be impossible to use after the first year of annuity payouts, as the annuity would have no "12/31/prior year" balance. A corollary to this rule, which is sometimes unrecognized by advisors, is that the payments from an IRA annuity in payout status satisfy *only* the RMD requirements *for that annuity*. They may *not* be applied against the RMD for the taxpayer's other IRA accounts.

If the annuity is *not* in payout status, the account balance of the annuity as of December 31st of the year preceding a Required Minimum Distribution must be increased by the actuarial value of additional contract benefits (including the value of "guaranteed living benefit" and "guaranteed minimum death benefit" riders[30]. There are two exceptions to this rule:

1. If the only additional benefit is a "return of premium" death benefit, that benefit is disregarded for purposes of this requirement[31].
2. If the total additional benefits are worth 20% or less of the annuity account value and are reduced, pro rata, by any distributions taken under those benefits, they are disregarded[32].

Note: While many "guaranteed living benefit" riders may qualify for this exception (especially, where contract performance has been so favorable that the "living benefit" guarantee is either not "in the money" or is only slightly greater than the contract would provide absent the guarantee), many such riders *do not* provide that withdrawals will result in "pro-rata" reductions in the guarantee value, but specify that reductions will be made on a "dollar for dollar" basis for at least a portion of those withdrawals.

It is possible that the application of this requirement (that additional benefits be added to account value for RMD purposes) could produce an RMD that exceeds the value of the annuity contract!

Example: Fred's IRA annuity has a cash value of $400,000. The **guaranteed minimum death benefit** *is $600,000 (perhaps due to good contract performance followed by poor performance). If Fred takes a* **partial withdrawal** *or makes a* **partial 1035 exchange** *[see "Partial Exchanges of an Annuity", above] of $398,000, and his contract provides that the guaranteed minimum death benefit will be reduced* **dollar for dollar** *by withdrawals (so that his resulting death benefit will be $202,000), he may expect that his Required Minimum Distribution will be based on the resulting contract value of $2,000. If, however, Fred is old enough that the actuarial value of that guaranteed death benefit increases the fair market value of the annuity substantially, his actual RMD could exceed the cash value of the contract!*

How is one to know the actuarial value of these additional benefits? Many insurers will calculate these values and provide them to contract owners. Where the insurer does not do so, see the examples in Treas. Reg. 1.401(a)(9)-6, A-12.

Determining the value of an IRA annuity for purposes of a Roth conversion

The value of an annuity held in an IRA must be increased by those additional benefits for purposes of determining the contract's fair market value for a conversion to a Roth IRA[33].

The final Treasury Regulations issued on Sept. 22nd, 2008[34] specify three methods for determining the fair market value of a Traditional IRA for Roth conversion purposes. They are:

1. *Gift Tax Method.* If the issuer of the annuity in question offers a "comparable contract" the price of that contract may be used. If the conversion occurs shortly after the annuity in question was purchased, the cost of the annuity in question may be used.

2. *Reserve Method.* If there is no comparable contract available, the fair market value may be established through an approximation that is based on the interpolated terminal reserve at the date of the conversion, plus the proportionate part of the gross premium last paid before the date of the conversion which covers the period extending beyond that date.

3. *Accumulation Method.* The annuity may be valued using the same methodology employed for determining Required Minimum Distributions (discussed above). However, for Roth conversion valuation purposes, there is no *de minimus* exception, so that benefit that are less than 20% of the contract value must be included. This method requires that all front-end loads and other non-recurring charges assessed in the twelve months immediately preceding the conversion be added to the account value.

---

1 At the time of this writing, there is one variable deferred annuity provision which guarantees the buyer the right to take distributions in the form of partial withdrawals (that is, other than by electing an "annuity payout option") and where such distributions will be taxed as "amounts received as an annuity" (per PLRs 200921039 and 201048044), so long as those distributions are made subject to the restrictions of that provision. This is a very unusual provision; partial withdrawals made from nearly all deferred annuity contracts will not receive this treatment, and

the 1099R forms prepared by their issuers will show those distributions as "amounts not received as an annuity". However, recent Private Letter Rulings issued with respect to "contingent annuities" have held that the withdrawals under these contracts would be treated as "amounts received as an annuity". PLRs 200949007, 201001016, 201129029; see Chapter 1, p. 11

2 PLRs 200818018, 200951039

3 PLR 201129029. See also PLRS 200949007, 201001016

4 IRC Sect. 72(e)(5)

5 If contributions to a non-natural person owed annuity were made after 2/28/1986, the §72(u) rules apply. If no contributions were made after that date, the contract will be treated as "an annuity". It is unclear how a contract containing contributions from both periods will be treated.

6 See PLRs 9204010, 9204014, 20049011, 9752035 (multi-beneficiary trust)

7 PLRs 200018046, 200720004

8 J. Gary Underwood, "Trust Ownership of Nonqualified Annuities: General Consideration for Trustees", Journal of Financial Service Professionals, May, 2010

9 PLR 199944020

10 IRC Sects. 72(e)(2)(B) and 72(e)(3)(A)

11 IRC Sects. 72(e)(5)(E) and §72(e)(5)(A)

12 IRC Sect. 72(e)(5)(A)(ii)

13 It should be noted that many insurers do not agree with this analysis, maintaining that the "without regard to surrender charge" element of IRC Section 72(e)(3)(A) applies to all non-annuitized distributions, full or partial. This is curious, given not only the clear exception for full surrenders of Section 72(e)(5)(A), but the IRS' own analysis in Private Letter Ruling 200030013, which includes the following: "Section 72(e)(5)(E) provides a statutory exception to section 72(e)(2)(A). The rule of section 72(e)(2)(A) is not applicable if the amount received is "under a contract on its complete surrender, redemption, or maturity." Section 72(e)(5)(A) provides that in situations in which paragraph (e)(5) applies, then paragraphs (2)(B) and (4)(A) shall not apply and if paragraph (2)(A) does not apply, then the amount distributed shall be included in gross income, but only to the extent that it exceeds the investment in the contract (basis-first rule). The basis-first rule provides that the taxpayer does not have to include any amounts into income to the extent that it does not exceed the taxpayer's investment in the contract".

43

Chapter 2: Taxation During Lifetime

14 IRC Sect. 165

15 Tax Facts, 2011, Vol. 2, Q. 3526, Q 3528

16 Rev. Rul. 61- 201, 1961-2 CB 46; Cohan v. Comm., 39 F.2d 540 (2nd Cir. 1930), aff'g 11 BTA 743

17 Rev. Rul. 92-95, 1992-2 C.B. 43

18 Treasury General Information letter, issued 6/29/2001

19 J. Gary Underwood, Ibid,, footnote 45

20   IRC Sects. 1035(d)(1), 1031(b)

21   IRC Sects. 1035(d)(1), 1031(c)

22 Conway v. Commissioner, 111 T.C. 350 (1998) , acq., 1999-2 C.B xvi
23 IRC Sect. 72(e)(4)(C)

24 PLR 201124008

25 First Nat'l Bank of Kansas City v. Comm., 309 F.2d 587 (8th Cir. 1962) aff'g Katz v. Comm., TC Memo 1961-270; Roff v. Comm., 304 F.2d 450 (3rd Cir. 1962) aff'g 36 TC 818; Arnfeld v. U.S., 163 F. Supp. 865 (Ct. Cl. 1958), cert. denied 359 U.S. 943

26 Another way of expressing "in payout status" is "after Annuity Starting Date"

27 Tax Facts 2011, Vol. 2, Q 3528

28 Mark L. Ascher, "The Grantor Trust Rules Should Be Repealed", Iowa Law Review, vol. 96, p. 885, 2011

29 Treas. Reg. 1.401(a)(9)-6, A-2

30 Treas. Reg. 1.401(a)(9)-6, A-12(a) & (b)

31 Treas. Reg. 1.401(a)(9)-6, A-12(c)

32 Treas. Reg. 1.401(a)(9)-6, A-12(c)

33 Treas. Reg. 1.408A-4, Q&A-14(a)

34 Internal Revenue Bulletin 2008-38

Chapter Three: Taxation Of Annuities After Death

The taxation of after-death distributions from nonqualified annuities is not an easy subject, even for those trained in tax law. One must know, not only how those distributions will be taxed, but also how, when, to whom, and over what period of time post-death distributions must be made in the first place. Some of the rules are not clear and some provisions of the Internal Revenue Code seem to conflict with other provisions (e.g.: how long may a beneficiary wait before electing to take death proceeds as an annuity without becoming in "constructive receipt" of the entire balance? IRC §72(h) says one thing; §72(s)(2) seems to say something else).

Fortunately, some of the rules are fairly straightforward, such as the rules for *estate* taxation of death proceeds.

Estate Taxation of Annuity

Whether an annuity is subject to *estate tax* depends, first, upon whether the annuity has any value following the owner's death. If not, there is no estate tax implication. (The estate tax is a tax on the right to transfer property; if there is nothing to transfer, there is no tax). If there is value remaining at owner's death, the tax treatment depends upon whether the annuity was in "payout status".

When the Annuity was in "Payout Status" and value remains in the contract, the remaining value is includible in the owner's estate.

Estate Taxation of Annuities "In Payout Status"

Annuity with a "Refund Feature"

If the decedent owner was receiving payments (as the annuitant) under an annuity option with a "refund feature" (that is, a guarantee of payment if the annuitant died prior to the expiry of a specified period, or before the amount annuitized had been paid out to the annuitant), the value of the refund feature is includible in decedent owner's estate.

Example 1: Fred was receiving payments under a "life and 120 months certain" annuity option. Fred died after receiving 50 monthly payments. The remaining 70 monthly payments will be paid to Fred's beneficiary. The value of those payments, includible in Fred's estate, is what the issuing insurer would charge for a 70 month "period certain" annuity[1].

Example 2: Same facts, except that Fred had elected a "life and cash refund" payout option. In this case, the amount due the beneficiary (the cash refund amount – which is usually less than the amount placed under annuitization) is presumably what will be includible in Fred's estate.

Joint and Survivor Annuity

If Fred was receiving payments under a Joint and Survivor annuity payout (regardless of whether the contract was an immediate annuity or a deferred annuity annuitized under that payout arrangement), the amount includible in Fred's estate depends upon who paid for the contract and whether the joint annuitants were a married couple.

- If Fred and the joint annuitant were married, the value of the survivor's annuity should qualify for the estate tax marital deduction.

- If Fred and the joint annuitant were not married, the value of the survivor's annuity is includible in Fred's estate to the extent that Fred paid for the contract[2].

If the value of the survivor annuity generates Federal estate tax at the death of the first owner/annuitant, the surviving annuitant may be entitled to a deduction for *a portion of* the tax paid (basically, the estate tax paid, less the excludible portion of payments to the surviving annuitant[3].

Estate Taxation of Annuity NOT "In Payout Status"

"An annuity not in payout status" refers to a *deferred* annuity contract where the owner has not yet elected to *annuitize* the contract under a regular annuity payout option. The estate taxation of such a contract is simple: The *death benefit* is fully includible in the decedent *owner's* estate. If the decedent was the *annuitant* but not the *owner*, there is no inclusion, because decedent did not own the property.

Deferred Annuities *Generally* Receive No "Step Up In Basis"

With only one exception, a deferred annuity *does not* receive a "step up in basis" at the death of the owner (IRC Section 1014). The exception is *variable* annuity contracts issued prior to October 21, 1979. Those contracts, to the extent of contributions made prior to that date and earnings allocable to such contributions, will enjoy an adjustment in basis, to the fair market value of the annuity as of the date of owner's death, for purposes of calculating the *beneficiary's* cost basis[4]. However, a contract acquired in a tax free exchange (under IRC §1035(a)) *will not* be "grandfathered", and will, therefore, be treated as any other deferred annuity (that is: beneficiary will inherit decedent owner's basis and contract value in excess of that amount will be "income in respect of a decedent")[5].

Beneficiary's Tax Deduction for Federal Estate Tax Attributable to Gain in Decedent's Deferred Annuity

As we have noted, the full value of an annuity, including the "gain" therein" owned by a decedent is includible in that decedent's estate for *estate tax* purposes. As the beneficiary will be liable for *income tax* on that same "gain", the result would be that the same dollars would be taxed twice at the Federal level. Some relief is provided by the "income in respect of a decedent" rules of IRC

Section 691(c). The beneficiary is entitled to a Federal *income tax* deduction for the *Federal* Estate Tax attributable to that "gain". This relief will not necessarily eliminate double taxation, as no deduction is granted for any *State* death tax attributable to that gain and the Federal deduction is available only if the beneficiary itemizes deductions.

Income Taxation of Annuity Death Benefits

The *income* tax treatment of annuity death benefits, both for contracts in payout status and those not in payout status, is governed by Section 72 of the Internal Revenue Code – chiefly, *but not entirely*, by Subsection 72(s) – and corresponding Treasury Regulations.

As noted at the outset of this chapter, much of the difficulty experienced by advisors trying to "understand the rules" flows from the fact that one must understand both the rules governing how a post-death distribution is taxed and the rules governing when such a distribution must be made. The latter is particularly important to legal and tax advisors whose clients include beneficiaries of nonqualified annuities wishing to know "what their options are".

Income Taxation of an Annuity in Payout Status – The "At Least As Rapidly As" Rule

IRC §72(s)(1)(A) states that –
"if any holder of such contract dies on or after the annuity starting date and before the entire interest in such contract has been distributed, the remaining portion of such interest will be distributed at least as rapidly as under the method of distributions being used as of the date of his death."

Put simply, this means that a beneficiary of an annuity in payout status may not "stretch" receipt of the death benefit over a period longer than the period over which the owner was taking payments.[6] A shorter payout is permissible.

A Curious Incongruity

When a beneficiary elects to continue taking payments in accordance with the schedule under which the deceased annuitant was receiving them (e.g.: continuing monthly payments over the remaining "refund period"), a curious switch in the taxation of those payments occurs. The "exclusion ratio" treatment, under which a portion of each payment to the deceased annuitant was excludible from income, no longer applies. Instead, the post-death annuity payments will be fully excludible from beneficiary's income until the total amount received by the beneficiary, when added to the tax-free amounts received by the annuitant, equal the owner's adjusted basis in the contract[7]. If the total payments thus made (both to the owner and the beneficiary) are less than the owner's adjusted basis, the beneficiary is entitled to an income deduction for that unrecovered investment[8].

Explanatory Note: In the above paragraph (and elsewhere in this book), the term "annuitant" is used to refer to the individual receiving annuity payments. However, the annuitant, as we noted in Chapter 1, is merely the "measuring life" of an annuity contract and may not be the individual who actually receives annuity payments. When the owner and annuitant are the same individual (as is usually, but not always, the case), this usage produces no confusion. However, the owner and annuitant are not always the same person, and, as we will see later in this chapter, that condition can produce unexpected results.

To make matters even more confusing, the Internal Revenue Code and Regulations, as well as some commonly used reference sources, sometimes use the term "annuitant" to refer to the taxpayer who owns the annuity. This is especially true of older Code sections and Regulations, drafted when all annuities paid a death benefit upon the death of the annuitant (so that the tax treatment of post-death distributions was always triggered by the death of the annuitant).

Example: *Tax Facts* 2011, Q. 3518, in describing the tax treatment of continuing annuity payments made to a beneficiary from

49

an annuity that had been in payout status (the scenario described above in "A Curious Incongruity"), states the rule as follows:

> *The beneficiary will have no taxable income until the total amount the beneficiary receives, when added to amounts that were received tax-free by the annuitant (the excludable portion of the annuity payments), exceeds the investment in the contract. In other words, all amounts received by the beneficiary are exempt from tax until the investment in the contract has been recovered tax-free; thereafter, receipts (if any) are taxable income.*

Clearly, this would not be literally correct if the annuitant were someone other than the contract owner. However, a correction might be even more confusing. It is probably sufficient for us to note that some sources (including the various components of "tax law") sometimes use the term "annuitant" when the rule being prescribed is obviously intended to apply to the taxpayer who *owns* the annuity. While we're at it, we should note that the Code and Regulations generally use the term "holder", rather than "owner" to describe the person or entity that owns an annuity.

Income Taxation of an Annuity **Not** in Payout Status

Advisors having to deal with post-death annuity tax questions will most often be dealing with contracts *not* in payout status for two reasons: First, most deferred annuities are never annuitized. Second, many immediate annuities terminate, at the death of the annuitant, with no death benefit (either because the payout option did not include a "refund feature" or because the annuitant outlived it).

The tax treatment that will apply to post-death annuity distributions is actually fairly simple. Here are three "rules of thumb":

1. To the extent that a distribution is includible in income, it is *always* taxed as ordinary income.

2. A penalty tax, assessed by IRC §72(q) will *always* apply unless the distribution qualifies for one of ten exceptions (see Chapter 2).
3. Distributions – either before or after death - from *nonqualified* contracts will *never* be taxable to the extent that such distributions represent a return of the owner's *investment in the contract* (i.e.: adjusted basis).

What's much less simple is the question of when, to whom, and over what period *post-death* distributions must be made as a matter of law. Section 72(s) of the Code (entitled *"Required Distributions Where Holder Dies Before Entire Interest Is Distributed."*) and the corresponding Regulations are the chief sources of answers here (although §72(h) is arguably relevant, however much it has been ignored of late [see discussion below]). But before we can examine what the Code and Regulations require, we must consider a question at the level of the annuity contract itself – namely –

Whose death triggers a death benefit, and, if there is more than one death benefit payable from a contract, whose death triggers which benefit?

"Annuitant-driven" vs. "Owner-driven" Annuities

The answer to that question depends upon (a) whether the contract is "annuitant-driven" and, if it is, on the identity of the decedent. The term "annuitant-driven" describes a deferred annuity contract (remember that we're talking, in this section of the chapter, about annuities "not in payout status" – that is: *deferred* annuities that have not been annuitized) that provides for payment of a death benefit upon the death of the *annuitant*.

"Owner Driven" contracts

The term "owner-driven" refers to a contract providing for a death benefit upon the death of the contract *owner*. This would suggest, to most English speakers, that a contract is either the one or the other – that a death benefit is payable *either* by reason of the death of the annuitant *or* by reason of the owner's death. That would make sense, but it's not quite correct because *all deferred annuity contracts issued since January 18th, 1985, are "owner-driven"* – *because §72(s)(1)(B) requires them to be*. That subsection states that no annuity contract will be treated as an "annuity contract" (and, thus, subject to the tax rules of §72) unless it provides that –

> *if any holder of such contract dies before the annuity starting date, the entire interest in such contract will be distributed within 5 years after the death of such holder.*

What does "Holder" Mean?

Note the word "holder". The whole of §72(s) refers to what provisions must be included in an annuity contract "where *holder* dies". It does not apply if someone other than the "holder" (such as a non-owner annuitant) dies. Moreover, "holder" is not as straightforward a label as it might appear. Generally speaking, it refers to the *owner* named in the annuity contract, but not always. When a deferred annuity is owned by a "non-natural person" (an entity other than a human being), §72(s)(6)(A) states that the *primary annuitant* shall be deemed to be the "holder", even if the owner designated in the annuity contract is someone else. As if that were not complicated enough, there are fact situations in which the individual who will be deemed to be the "holder" is not entirely clear, such as when an annuity, of which B is named as primary annuitant, is owned by A's irrevocable grantor trust (see discussion in Chapter 4 "Annuities and Trusts").

Some contracts are *also* "annuitant-driven"

Some deferred annuity contracts, *in addition to* being "owner-driven" (because they must be, to be considered "annuity contracts") are *also* "annuitant-driven". That is, they offer *a* death benefit upon the death of the *annuitant. In some contracts, that death benefit is not necessarily the same as the death benefit that will be payable upon the death of the owner.* For example, some contracts offer an "enhanced" or "guaranteed minimum" death benefit that may be greater than the contract value. When that benefit is payable upon the death of the *annuitant*, there are actually two death benefits in the contract – the "enhanced", or *guaranteed minimum,* death benefit, payable when the annuitant dies, and the contract value, that must be paid out upon the death of the owner. Obviously, this is never an issue when the owner and annuitant are the same individual. But when they're not, problems can result.

Annuitant-driven contract: Where owner and annuitant are not the same individual

Example: John owned a variable deferred annuity, of which his wife, Jane, was named annuitant. The contract included a guaranteed minimum death benefit, payable on annuitant's death, equal to the greatest of (a) the contract value at death, or (b) the contract value at any policy anniversary prior to death, or (c) total contributions to the annuity, accumulated at X%[9]. The beneficiary of the annuity was John's revocable living trust.

At Jane's death, the trust would receive that "enhanced" death benefit. But what if John died first? The trust would receive only the contract value (less any surrender charges or "Market Value Adjustment", if applicable). Why? Because the owner died, and the contract provided that, at the death of the owner, the contract value would be paid (per IRC §72(s)(1)(B)). As Jane, the annuitant, did not die, the guaranteed minimum death benefit would not be payable.

Clearly, there is opportunity for confusion as to *who will get what benefit* when the owner and annuitant are different individuals and where the contract provides for two death benefits (which occurs *only* in "annuitant-driven" contracts where annuitant and owner are not the same individual). But there is also opportunity for even more distressing results.

Example: Grandma Goodman has become dissatisfied with the interest she's earning on her Certificate of Deposit. When Joe, an insurance agent, calls her, recommending a deferred annuity currently earning a higher rate, she says

Chapter 3: Taxation After Death

"come on over". As Joe is completing the insurance application, he learns that she is 81 years old. Knowing that his insurance company will not accept applications for deferred annuities where the *annuitant* is over age 80, Joe suggests that Grandma name her daughter, Gretchen, as annuitant. "That's just a formality, Grandma", he says. "You're the owner, and it's your property. As long as you're alive, the money in this annuity is yours, whenever you want it." (*We'll ignore, for this example, the fact that the surrender charges in the annuity contract may restrict, perhaps for a long time, Grandma's access to those contract values*).

If the contract **is not** *annuitant-driven*, Gretchen will be merely the "measuring life" (whose life expectancy will determine the size of any annuity payouts if Grandma elects to annuitize). Gretchen's death *may* have no impact. Most sources state that Grandma can name a new annuitant, and most insurers will permit same. Indeed, many newer annuitant-driven contracts now state that the owner is deemed to be contingent annuitant (*see "Company B" example below*).

If the contract **is** *annuitant-driven*, Gretchen's death will cause payout of all contract values to the named beneficiary within five years (under §72(s)(1)(B), unless an exception occurs. (We'll get to the exceptions shortly). If Grandma is both owner and beneficiary, she'll get her money, but she'll have to pay tax on any "gain" in the contract.

But what if Grandma designates a third party (someone other than herself or the annuitant) as beneficiary? This is a recipe for *disaster!*

First, Gretchen's death will usually cause the entire contract value to be paid out to that named beneficiary, despite Joe's assurance to Grandma that she would always have control of the money in the annuity. (See below for examples of contract language that would alter this result).

Second, the entire gain in the contract will be taxable to the beneficiary as "income in respect of a decedent"[10].

Third, the death benefit would *not* meet the "distributions on account of death" exception to the 10% penalty tax, because that exception (§72(q)(2)(B)) is available only when the distribution is made "on or after the death of the *holder*. Gretchen (the non-owner annuitant) died, not Grandma (the owner).

Fourth, Grandma will be deemed to have made a *gift* of the death benefit to the beneficiary[11].

It should be noted that while this result has occurred in annuitant-driven annuities, it seldom happens, for several reasons: First, because most annuities are not annuitant-driven; second, because most buyers of deferred annuity contracts desire to be both owner and annuitant; third, because many (but, regrettably, not all) agents are aware of the "trap" and will advise annuity buyers against making the annuitant and beneficiary designations that trigger it; and fourth, because many insurers have inserted language in their annuitant-driven contract to prevent the occurrence of this "Goodman triangle trap". A variable deferred annuity issued by Company B states -

> *If an annuitant who is not the contract owner or joint owner dies, then the contingent annuitant, if named, becomes the annuitant and no death benefit is payable on the death of the annuitant. If no contingent annuitant is named, the contract owner (or younger of joint owners) becomes the annuitant.*

Thus, although that contract is "annuitant-driven", the death of a *non-owner* annuitant does not trigger payment of a death benefit. Not all insurers, however, include such language. Company A's index annuity contract includes the following:

> *"Death of non-owner annuitant: We will pay the Beneficiary the Death Benefit provided in your contract if the Annuitant who is not an Owner dies before the Annuity Date while your contract is in effect."*

Chapter 3: Taxation After Death

If the beneficiary of that contract is someone other than the annuitant (which one would expect to be the case, as it is the death of the annuitant that triggers payment of the death benefit) or the owner, the result would be our "Grandma Goodman" tax disaster. (It may be that Company A would not permit issuance of the contract in that case, but there is nothing in the language of the application or contract that guarantees it).

But what if the owner of an annuitant-driven contract, who is not the annuitant, dies (before Annuity Starting Date)? As we've seen, IRC 72(s) requires payout within five years (unless an exception applies). Many contracts provide that, in that situation, payment will be made to the named beneficiary. Company A's index annuity contract creates a party called the "designated beneficiary", (who is *not* the beneficiary named in the contract) who will receive the proceeds only upon the death of a contract owner who is not the annuitant. The "designated beneficiary" is the contingent owner named in the application or, if none, a joint owner, *or, if none, the owner's estate!* Upon the death of an annuitant who is also the owner, the death benefit is payable to the "regular" beneficiary.

One might question whether an applicant for Company A's annuity (or the agent selling it) will understand that the death of the annuitant will result in a payment to the party named as beneficiary, but that the death of a non-annuitant owner will trigger payment to the contingent owner (or owner's estate).

The application for an annuity issued by another insurer ("Company C") takes a third approach, including entries for "Owner's beneficiary" and "Annuitant's beneficiary". This might easily produce a "triangle trap" result, unless Company C's application processing policies would prevent issuance of such an application.

As we have seen, the designation of owner, annuitant, and beneficiary should be made with great care. The agent completing an application *should* be fully aware of the consequences of these designation decisions, but that is not always the case. The insurance company processing an application where owner, annuitant, and beneficiary are three different parties *may* have in place policies to delay issuance unless it is satisfied that the applicant is fully aware of the consequences, but, in the author's experience, most insurers do not. This places a serious burden upon any advisor (attorney, accountant, trust officer, financial planner, etc.) who is called upon to review a client's annuity.

Now that we've seen how a deferred annuity contract can have more than one death benefit, and the problems that can arise when the owner and annuitant are not the same individual, let's return to the general rules governing when a death benefit must be payable from an annuity not in payout status.

Section 72(s)(1)(B) – The "Five Year Rule". We noted earlier that Section 72(s)(1)(B) requires that, upon death of the holder, the entire value of the contract must be paid out over five years unless an exception applies. This is the *default* rule, which will govern unless either of two exceptions applies:

Section 72(s)(2) - *Where there is a "designated beneficiary" named in the annuity contract,* that individual may elect to take death proceeds *as an annuity*, over a period not extending beyond his or her life expectancy[12]. A *life annuity* is not required, only that the annuity cannot extend beyond the beneficiary's life expectancy.

Section 72(s)(3) – "Spousal continuation" when the designated beneficiary is the surviving spouse of the holder. Under this exception, the surviving spouse/beneficiary may elect to treat the annuity as his or her own, as if he or she were the original purchaser, and exercise all ownership options (including continuing the contract in force).

These two exceptions are not quite as simple as they may first appear. For example, neither exception applies unless the annuity is payable to, or for the benefit of, a "designated beneficiary". What does that term mean? It means "any ***individual*** designated a beneficiary by the holder of the contract"[13]. "Individual" means *human being*. A trust, for example, is not an individual, and therefore, in the strictest sense, cannot be a "designated beneficiary". However, tax authorities and insurers disagree as to whether one needs to read the first exception quite so literally. In the next chapter, we will consider whether a trust, named as beneficiary of an annuity, *where that trust is for the benefit of an individual who would, if named directly, qualify as a "designated beneficiary,* may qualify for the "annuitization" exception of Section 72(s)(2).

Assuming, for the sake of discussion, that an individual is named as beneficiary, what requirements must that individual satisfy in order to qualify for the "annuity" exception of 72(s)(2)?

The first exception to the "Five Year Rule" – Annuitization by the Beneficiary (§72(s)(2))

Section 72(s)(2) states that -
*If—
(A) any portion of the holder's interest is payable to (or for the benefit of) a designated beneficiary,
(B) such portion will be distributed (in accordance with regulations) over the life of such designated beneficiary (or over a period not extending beyond the life expectancy of such beneficiary), and
(C) such distributions begin not later than 1 year after the date of the holder's death or such later date as the Secretary may by regulations prescribe,*

We've assumed that (A) is true and we will further assume that the beneficiary elects to take payments over a period not extending beyond his or her life expectancy (meeting requirement (B)). The third requirement (C) states that the income payments must commence not later than one year after holder's death[14].

Does this mean that the beneficiary must make the election to take death proceeds as an annuity within one year of the owner's death? It would appear so, but this, too, is not quite so clear, for two reasons: First, because requirement (C) does not speak to when the election must be made, but only to when the first income payment must commence, and, second, because a provision of tax law a generation older than Section 72(s) is still "on the books", one which speaks directly to when such election must be made, and which mandates a much shorter election period.

The Strange Case of Section 72(h)

Section 72(h) is entitled "Option To Receive An Annuity In Lieu Of A Lump Sum". It states that –

If —

(1) a contract provides for payment of a lump sum in full discharge of an obligation under the contract, subject to an option to receive an annuity in lieu of such lump sum;

(2) the option is exercised within 60 days after the day on which such lump sum first became payable; and

(3) part or all of such lump sum would (but for this subsection) be includible in gross income by reason of subsection (e) (1),

then, for purposes of this subtitle, no part of such lump sum shall be considered as includible in gross income at the time such lump sum first became payable.

This means that if the language of a deferred annuity contract permits that contract to be paid out in the form of an annuity (in lieu of a lump sum payment) and if the option of the payee to take such an annuity is exercised within sixty days, and if some or all of the annuity proceeds would otherwise be includible in the payee's income (that is, would not be eligible for the exclusion afforded by IRC Section 101(a) to *life insurance* proceeds) the payee will not be considered to be in "constructive receipt" of the entire proceeds (and, thus, liable for tax on all the gain in that contract).

This would appear to say that the payee has sixty days to elect "annuitization". Why do we say "payee", here, rather than "beneficiary"? Because Section 72(h) does not speak only to death proceeds, but to *any* proceeds of an annuity that could be paid out either in a lump sum or in the form of an annuity. It applies equally well to an annuity that is about to mature for a lump sum, but which provides the *living* contract owner with the option to take proceeds as an annuity. In the present case, however, we are concerned only with death proceeds - that is, where the death of *someone* will cause payout of the annuity. That *someone* could be either the contract owner or a non-owner annuitant, if the annuity is "annuitant-driven".

So, it appears that, while Section 72(s)(2) requires only that the first payment of an annuity (chosen by a beneficiary in lieu of a lump sum payout or payout over five years [per Section 72(s)(1)(B)]) *commence* within *one year* of the contract owner's death, Section 72(h) requires the beneficiary to elect such annuity payout within *sixty days*.

But sixty days *from when?* Many authorities believe that this means "sixty days from the death that triggered the payout". *But that is not what 72(h) actually says.* It says that the election to take payout as an annuity must be exercised "*within 60 days after the day on which such lump sum first became payable*". When does the death benefit of a deferred annuity first become payable? The author believes that it is at least arguable that this date is the first day in which the issuer of the annuity would approve payment of that death benefit to that beneficiary. No insurer will approve such payment unless and until it has received the required paperwork, including a death certificate and a properly completed "death claim form" signed by the beneficiary. The 60 day "annuity election period" of 72(h) could, therefore, mean "sixty days from the date the insurer receives the election". But that is nonsensical; a time restriction requiring a beneficiary to elect an option no later than sixty days from the date on which that beneficiary filed the paperwork for that very election would have no force.

Perhaps this is why almost everyone has been ignoring Section 72(h) for years. The author has been unable to find any case law in which the IRS has ruled, either for or against, an annuity beneficiary's "late election" and cited Section 72(h) in its decision. There are, however, many court cases and Private Letter Rulings addressing the "annuity payments must commence within *one year*" requirement of Section 72(s)(2). Deferred annuity contracts often state that a beneficiary must elect annuity payout within sixty days, but the *company practice* of many, if not most, insurers is to permit such election so long as the first annuity payment is made within one year of death – of either the owner or the annuitant (in the case of an annuitant-driven contract).

What can one make of this strange incongruity of requirements? The author believes that the prudent advisor will counsel a beneficiary to decide how to receive annuity death proceeds as soon as possible *because Section 72(h) is still "on the books"*. However, as most insurers will permit a tardy election – and, more importantly, will issue Forms 1099-R to beneficiaries reflecting a timely election – a "late filing" may not be cause for panic.

The second exception to the "Five Year Rule" – "Spousal Continuation" (§72(s)(3))

A beneficiary of an annuity who is the surviving spouse of the *owner* has another option (in addition to taking proceeds as an annuity under 72(s)(2)) – treating the annuity as if he or she were the original purchaser and owner. That surviving spouse may choose to continue the annuity (which is why this provision is usually called the "spousal continuation" option) or do anything else with it that an owner may do (including surrendering it, taking of partial withdrawals, annuitizing the contract, and naming beneficiaries). This option is available *only* when the death benefit of the annuity is paid out by reason of the death of the contract *owner, and* when the beneficiary is that owner's surviving spouse. It is *not* available when a *non-owner annuitant* has died, even when the beneficiary is that annuitant's surviving spouse, nor is it available when the owner dies and the beneficiary is a trust for the benefit of owner's spouse (as we will discuss in the next chapter).

Example: George owns, and is beneficiary of, an "annuitant-driven" deferred annuity, of which Gracie, George's wife, is the annuitant. If Gracie dies, the contract will pay a death benefit (the "enhanced death benefit", if the contract provides for one) to George. George may elect to take that death benefit (a) in a lump sum; (b) over five years (§72(s)(1)(B)); or (c) as an annuity not extending beyond his life expectancy (§72(s)(2)). He *may not* continue the contract as his own (per §72(s)(3)) because he is not the surviving spouse of the *owner*.

Chapter 3: Taxation After Death

Having examined when a beneficiary (surviving spouse or not) may elect to receive death proceeds as an annuity, let's look at how those annuity payments will be taxed.

We noted, in Chapter 2, that all distributions from any annuity, whether made to a living annuity owner or to a beneficiary, are either *amounts received as an annuity* or *amounts not received as an annuity*. The former are taxed under the "regular annuity rules" of Section 72(b), where part of each payment is excluded from the recipient's income as a return of principal. When the beneficiary elects an *annuity payout option* (a life annuity, with or without a "refund element" *or* a "period certain annuity) under the contract, payments under that option qualify as "amounts received as an annuity" and get that "regular annuity rules" treatment. The *exclusion ratio* (that determines the amount of each annuity payment that is excluded from the beneficiary's income) is calculated using the deceased annuitant's remaining adjusted basis (*"investment in the contract"*) and the beneficiary's life expectancy (adjusted by the value of any refund element).

Until fairly recently, this payout option – election of an annuity option that, for life annuities at least, is almost always irrevocable – was the only one that would qualify payments made thereunder as "amounts received as an annuity". However, in 2001, the IRS held, in a Private Letter Ruling[15], that a beneficiary of a deferred annuity contract who elected to receive the death benefit in payments made in accordance with the "Unified Table" used to determine Required Minimum Distributions from IRAs and qualified plans would not be held to be "in constructive receipt" of the undistributed contract gain. That Ruling did not, however, express an opinion as to whether the amounts thus received would qualify as "amounts received as an annuity".

Two years later, in another Private Letter Ruling[16], the IRS held that distributions made in accordance with that same arrangement (that is: made in accordance with the "life expectancy fraction method") would, "to the extent that they do not exceed the amounts required by such calculation, qualify as 'amounts received as an annuity'."

CAVEAT: Private Letter Rulings may be relied upon only by the taxpayer to whom they are issued; they are *not* "precedents". Moreover, the annuity contract referred to in the second PLR specified that the beneficiary electing the "fractional method" could choose to take any undistributed proceeds either (a) in a lump sum or (b) as additional partial withdrawals (in excess of those determined by that fractional method). The Ruling stated that only those beneficiaries who elected the first option would be entitled to "amounts received as an annuity" tax treatment with respect to the "fractional method" payouts.

Perhaps more importantly, it is irrelevant whether the IRS would grant "amounts received as an annuity" treatment to payments to a beneficiary made under the "fractional method" if the issuer of the annuity will not permit payouts on that basis. Not all annuity contracts permit this arrangement.

Jointly Held Annuities

Married individuals often prefer to own their investments jointly (either Jointly with Rights of Survivorship or Jointly By The Entireties). This can produce unforeseen results when the property in question is a deferred annuity because, while most property held in a joint tenancy passes, at the death of the first tenant, to the surviving tenant *as a matter of law*, the value of a deferred annuity, held jointly, may not do so. Often, the annuity value will pass to the named beneficiary, *even where a surviving owner still lives*, because it does so *as a matter of contract.*

Example: Abelard and Heloise, a married couple, purchase a deferred annuity in Joint Tenancy, with Right of Survivorship. Each is named as a Joint Owner. Believing that at the death of either spouse, the surviving spouse will continue as surviving owner, they name their church as beneficiary. Abelard dies, and Heloise requests the insurance company to adjust its records to reflect the fact that Heloise is now sole owner. She is shocked to receive a letter from that insurer informing her that the annuity death benefit will be paid to her church. She retains legal counsel to assert what she regards as her right to the annuity value (and the right to continue that contract as her own). After consulting an expert, her attorney informs her that her only option is to a representative of her church to disclaim, on behalf of the church, the annuity proceeds – which will, he says, result in payment of the death benefit to the annuity owner's estate (the default payee in that contract where no beneficiary exists at owner's death).

Why can this happen? (Actually, it *did* happen; the author was the expert retained by the widow's attorney). Because the death benefit must pass by the terms of the *contract*, which, in this case, stated that, at the death of *any* owner, the annuity death benefit would be paid to the beneficiary named in the contract.

Some annuity contracts contain language to preclude this result. For example, one major insurer, which will not issue a deferred annuity to be held jointly unless the joint owners are a married couple, includes in its contracts language stating that where the contract is owned jointly by spouses and one owner dies, the surviving spouse will be deemed to be Primary Beneficiary, notwithstanding any beneficiary designations to the contrary. Thus, on the death of either spouse, the surviving spouse will be entitled, not only to the death benefit, but to continue the contract (per §72(s)(3)) – not as surviving joint tenant, but as a primary beneficiary who is the surviving spouse of the deceased owner.

> Note: Payout from an annuity held by joint owners must be made upon the death of *either* owner because of a change in Section 72(s)(1) wrought by the Tax Reform Act of 1986. Prior to the change, that paragraph required payout upon the death of "*the* holder", which, according to some, meant that payout was not required until the death of the *last* holder (owner); it now reads "*any* holder" and clearly mandates payout upon the death of the *first* owner.

Even in the absence of contract language such as that cited above, joint purchasers of an annuity can achieve the same result by naming one another as primary beneficiary. But is that really necessary?

Annuity Taxation and Suitability for the Professional Advisor

Indeed, is joint ownership necessary? Often, couples wish that arrangement so that, upon the death of either, the survivor will be entitled to the annuity value without the expense and delay of Probate. Yet that result could be achieved simply by naming one spouse owner and annuitant and the other as beneficiary. On the death of either, the survivor would control the annuity (either as original owner or as surviving spouse/beneficiary, with the right to "spousal continuation").

1 Treas. Reg. §20.2031-8(a)

2 Treas. Reg. §20.2039-1(c), ex. 1

3 *Tax Facts* 2011, Vol 2, Q 3517, IRC §691(d)

Chapter 3: Taxation After Death

4 Rev. Rul. 79-335, 1979-2 CB 292

5 TAM 9346002; Let. Rul. 9245035

6 This requirement looks very much like the basic rule applying to payments to beneficiaries of IRAs and qualified plans (IRC §401(a)(9)(B)(i)), but, unlike that provision, it is to be taken literally. As Natalie Choate notes, the Treasury Regulations relating to §401(a)(9)(B)(i) have "administratively repealed" that Code section. The Required Minimum Distributions for a "designated beneficiary" of an IRA or qualified plan, and the Applicable Distribution Period over which those distributions must be taken are in no way related to either the amount of Required Minimum Distribution taken by the deceased participant or the period over which he or she was taking those distributions. (Natalie Choate, *Life and Death Planning for Retirement Benefits*, 7th edition, 2011, p. 67). The author cannot recommend this book highly enough. It is "the bible" for advisors offering advice in this area. The book is available at www.ataxplan.com.

7 Treas. Reg. §1.72-11(c)

8 IRC §72(b)(3)(A)

9 This is a fairly typical "enhanced" death benefit, available in many variable annuities. Some index annuities offer a somewhat similar guaranteed minimum death benefit – usually the greater of the contract value or contributions accumulated at a given rate of interest.

10 Some commentators have suggested that the tax liability is that of Grandma, as she is the taxpayer owning the contract and has not died; however, most authorities believe that the tax liability is that of the recipient, the beneficiary.

11 Goodman v. Comm'r, 156 F. 2nd 218 (1946)

12 IRC §72(s)(2)

13 IRC §72(s)(4)

14 We must bear in mind that Section 72(s) deals *only* with distributions from annuities that must be made after the death of the *holder* (owner); the death of a non-owner annuitant *will not* trigger application of any of these rules.

15 PLR 200151038

16 PLR 200313016

Chapter Four: Annuities and Trusts

The use of an annuity in financial and estate planning can be troublesome for two basic reasons: *Coordination* and *Taxation*.

Coordination of an annuity with the rest of the plan

Because the value of an annuity passes *by contract* rather than by will or trust or through intestacy law, the transfer of wealth that occurs when an annuity is paid out upon death may not be well coordinated with the rest of the wealth holder's plan. We've seen, in earlier chapters, that the value of an annuity may pass from the owner even while that owner is living (i.e.: if the annuity is "annuitant-driven" and the owner is neither the annuitant nor the beneficiary). Moreover, even when that is not the case (e.g.: when the wealth holder is both the owner and annuitant of the contract), the fact that the value of an annuity will pass to individuals named as beneficiaries irrespective of any formulas for "who get what" in the annuity owner's will or trust can produce results that may be inconsistent with the overall estate planning goals.

> *Example:* John and Jane, a married couple, have three children. They wish, at John's death, for half of John's assets to pass to Jane and the rest to be divided equally among the children. Their wills dictate that arrangement. If John owns a life insurance or annuity policy payable to Jane, the death benefit will pass to Jane over and above her share of John's other property (unless his estate planning documents take into account such a death benefit in calculating her share).

Financial and estate planners need to be aware of how beneficiary designations in annuity contracts (and life insurance policies, IRAs, qualified plans, and other instruments that pass wealth outside of the owner's will and trust(s)) will affect the overall plan.

Taxation of an annuity when it is owned by or is payable to a trust (or other "non-natural person)

While the tax rules applying to annuities are complicated enough under ordinary circumstances, they're even more complex and confusing when a trust is named as owner or beneficiary of a *deferred* annuity. Immediate annuities rarely present these problems because the tax provisions that create the most problems do not apply to immediate annuities. For that reason, we'll be focusing chiefly on deferred annuities; moreover, we'll be considering only *non-qualified* contracts (annuities not purchased inside qualified plans or IRAs) because, once again, the tax rules that create the problems and confusion do not apply to "qualified" contracts.

Before we go any further, the author would like to make a general observation at this point regarding annuities and trusts:

> ***Do not*** **name a trust as *either* owner *or* beneficiary of a trust unless you are (a) thoroughly familiar with the tax consequences of such a designation and (b) sure that the benefits of doing so outweigh any disadvantages (including those tax consequences).**

An obvious corollary to the above suggestion (which the author feels strongly enough about to present it as a *rule of thumb*) is that if you are asked to give advice regarding an annuity that is owned by or payable to a trust (or both), do not do so unless you fully understand the implications of that arrangement. With those caveats, let's look now at *why* the interaction of a deferred annuity and a trust can cause trouble.

There are three ways in which an annuity and a trust can interact:

1. The trust may own the annuity but not be the beneficiary
2. The trust may be the beneficiary, but not the owner, of an annuity

3. The trust may be both owner and beneficiary of the annuity

We will consider all three scenarios, but let's begin with a general consideration of the tax implications when a trust is named as owner of an annuity.

When an annuity is <u>owned by</u> a trust

As was discussed earlier, IRC Section 72(u) provides that a *deferred* annuity owned by a "non-natural person" (e.g.: a trust) will not enjoy the benefit of tax deferral unless an exception applies (see Chapter 2, pps 25-27)[1]. That section deals only with the taxation of an annuity "during lifetime" – that is, before the annuity must be paid out because someone has died.

But the rules that govern how the value of a deferred annuity must be paid out at death are also modified when the annuity owner is a trust. As we saw in Chapter 2, Section 72(s) requires that the entire value of the annuity must, *upon the death of any owner*, be paid out over five years [IRC Sect. 72(s)(1)(B)], unless payable to a human being (in which event, that beneficiary may elect to take distribution as an annuity over a period no longer than his/her life expectancy [IRC Sect. 72(s)(2)]). If he or she is also the surviving spouse of the owner, the "spousal continuation" exception is available [IR Sect. 72(s)(3)].

But trusts are not human beings and do not "die". (They may *terminate,* but that's not the same thing). If an annuity is owned by a trust, may that contract be continued indefinitely (or until the trust is terminated)? It may not. IRC Sect. 72(s)(6)(A) specifies that where the owner of a deferred annuity is a "corporation or other non-individual" (i.e.: not a human being), "the primary annuitant shall be treated as the holder of the contract". Thus, the death of the primary annuitant will be treated as the death of the owner, and the distribution requirements of Sect. 72(s)(1)(B), (2), and (3) will apply. This may appear, at first glance, to be a fairly straightforward rule, but it poses some difficult questions. We will examine some of these questions in the following scenarios.

69

Scenario 1: A trust owns a "non-annuitant driven" annuity

Trust A owns a deferred annuity, of which George is named primary annuitant. This particular annuity is not "annuitant-driven" (that is, it does not provide for payment of a death benefit upon the death of the annuitant). George dies. Sect. 72(s)(6)(A) tells us that the owner has died, and that the contract must be paid out. But suppose that the contract language of the annuity does not provide for such a payout because the owner designated in the contract has not died. Does the law "trump" the contractual provisions, requiring payout? If so, would any annuity surrender charges apply (that would be waived, under the contract upon the death of the owner named in the annuity) even though that named owner has not died?

Fortunately, this quandary is rarely encountered because many annuity contracts that are not "annuitant-driven" provide that when the owner is other than a natural person, the death benefit will be paid upon the death of the primary annuitant.

Scenario 2: An annuity is owned by an irrevocable grantor trust *and the grantor is not the annuitant*

George establishes an irrevocable grantor trust and the trust purchases a deferred annuity. The trust is named owner and beneficiary. The primary annuitant is George's daughter, Sally. Whose death triggers payout of the contract? The answer is not clear. Some authorities state that Sally's death must cause payout. Others insist that George's death must do so.

Does Sally's death trigger payout? IRC Sect. 72(s)(6)(A) declares that when an annuity is owned by a non-natural person, the primary annuitant shall be deemed, for purposes of post death distribution requirements, to be the holder (owner). Thus, the death of Sally, the imputed owner, will trigger payout under the provisions of Sect. 72(s). Of course, if the annuity contract is annuitant-driven, the contract will be paid out upon Sally's death (that is, the death of the annuitant) even if 72(s)(6)(A) were not implicated.

Does George's death trigger payout? Some authorities insist that the grantor trust rules require that the annuity be paid out upon George's death, even though George is neither the annuitant nor the owner named in the annuity contract or deemed owner by application of Sect. 72(s)(6)(A). Gary Underwood makes the case for this position in his excellent article entitled "Trust Ownership of Nonqualified Annuities: General Consideration for Trustees". He writes –

> "Alternatively, one might argue that the death of a nongrantor annuitant triggers the death distribution rules, even for grantor trusts. Although no authority explicitly addresses this issue, distribution at the death of the grantor is the most logical choice. Since the grantor is the owner of grantor trust assets for income tax purposes, and the death of the owner is the primary trigger for annuity distributions at death, then the death of the grantor should trigger the death distribution requirements. It seems incorrect to assert that the grantor is the owner of the annuity for income tax purposes, but the grantor is not the owner for the income tax requirement of distributions at death under IRC Sec. 72. Although some insurance companies treat the death of the grantor as a distribution event, it is possible that other insurance companies may not be aware of the death of a nonannuitant grantor and may not have reporting procedures in place to trigger a distribution"[2].

The author has been unable to find any authority as to which position is correct, or even any case law dealing with this issue. In practical terms, appears that the "correct" answer is whatever the issuing insurer decides is correct- *because that insurer will take action, or not take action, depending upon its interpretation.* If it is the policy of that insurer to distribute the value of the annuity on the death of the primary annuitant (as Sect. 72(s)(6)(A) mandates), it will make such distribution, and apply the restrictions of Sect. 72(s). This will happen even if Mr. Underwood's interpretation is correct, and it's the grantor's death that "should" trigger such payout. Moreover, if the trust is beneficiary of the annuity as well as the owner (which many insurers require), most insurers will require full distribution of the contract within five years.

If, on the other hand, the issuing insurer's policy follows Mr. Underwood's interpretation, it will *not* require payout upon Sally's death *unless the annuity is "annuitant-driven",* but *will* do so upon George's death. In conversations with representatives of several insurers, the author has learned that some insurers follow the rule of Sect. 72(s)(6)(A) and will require payout on George's death, while others agree with Mr. Underwood's interpretation (and will require payout if Sally dies first).

It is vital that everyone involved in such a scenario (in this case, George, Sally, the Trustee of George's trust, and all advisors offering counsel regarding the annuity) know, **before anyone dies,** *what the issuing insurer will require in the event of either George's or Sally's death.*

Scenario 3: An annuity is gifted to an irrevocable grantor trust

George establishes an irrevocable grantor trust and makes a gift of a deferred annuity, of which he is primary annuitant, to the trust. Is this a taxable transaction? For *gift* tax purposes, it clearly is. But is it a taxable event for *income* tax purposes? Here, too, we have an apparent contradiction between what the grantor trust rules would appear to dictate and the express requirements of a portion of IRC Sect. 72.

Sect. 72(e)(4)(C) states that "if an individual who holds an annuity contract transfers it without full and adequate consideration", that individual must recognize, as income, the "gain" in the contract in the year of such transfer. Those who assert that the grantor trust rules prevail in this scenario consider the gift of the annuity not to be a 'transfer" for *income* tax purposes because the same taxpayer is involved on both ends of the transaction and one cannot make a taxable transaction with oneself. Often, proponents of this position cite Rev. Rul. 85-13, 1985-1 C.B. 184[3]. However, that Revenue Ruling dealt with a grantor who acquired the corpus of a trust in exchange for that grantor's promissory note. The Service ruled that this acquisition of trust corpus by grantor did not constitute a sale for income tax purposes.

It is significant (in the author's opinion) that the Ruling cited Sect. 1.675-1 of the Income Tax Regulations, noting that that Section "treats the grantor as the owner of a trust if, under the terms of the trust instrument, or the circumstances attendant to its operation, administrative control is exercisable primarily for the benefit of the grantor rather than the beneficiaries of the trust". In reviewing the applicability of Sect. 675, the Ruling observed that "In all of these cases, the justification for treating the grantor as owner is evidence of *substantial grantor dominion and control over the trust*" [emphasis added].

In this author's opinion, such justification is arguably not present in our present scenario. Prior to making the gift, George could exercise unfettered control over the annuity; afterwards, he cannot. Control of the annuity has shifted, but not the tax liability. In this scenario, as in the situation described in Scenario 2, there is no clear authority in the Code, Regulations, or case law, so one is forced to make a guess as to which section of "the law" prevails. Underwood argues that the most common sensible approach would be to assume that the grantor trust provisions prevail, and that Sect. 72(e)(4)(C) simply doesn't apply because no transfer has taken place, *for income tax purposes*. This author is not so sure that the grantor trust provisions of the Code and Rev. Rul. 85-13 can be safely stretched to cover the facts of the present scenario and that the plain language rule of IRC. Sect. 72(e)(4)(C) can be ignored.

Scenario 4: An annuity is owned by a revocable living trust

Many clients believe that "everything needs to be in my living trust" and make ownership designations to achieve that result. When a non-qualified immediate annuity is transferred into a living trust or is purchased by one, the result can be both unforeseen and unfortunate (e.g.: if any of the trust beneficiaries is not a human being, the annuity will probably not qualify as "an annuity" for income tax purposes and earnings will be taxable as earned).

Sometimes, the result is desirable. For example, in the event of the client's becoming incapacitated or incompetent, trust provisions dealing with that situation may be more efficient than merely making the annuity subject to a Durable Power of Attorney. Often, however, little or nothing is gained by making the trust the *owner* of the annuity that would not be achieved by merely designating the trust as *beneficiary* (e.g.: The dispositive provisions of a trust can be "custom tailored", whereas most insurers will not accept highly complex beneficiary designations. If such "customization" is desirable, the annuity need only be *payable to* the trust).

Scenario 5: Annuity is owned by an irrevocable non-grantor trust

As the annuitant will be deemed to be the holder (under Sect. 72(s)(6)(A)), all distributions made during the lifetime of the annuitant will be subject to the 10% Sect. 72(q) penalty because none of the exceptions of Section 72(q)(2) can apply. The trust is the *taxpayer*, and it cannot become disabled (§72(q)(2)(C)) or attain age 59 ½ (§72(q)(2)(A)) and the deemed holder (the annuitant) has not died (§72(q)(2)(B)).

When an annuity is <u>payable to</u> a trust

In the author's experience, a trust is more frequently named as *beneficiary* of a deferred annuity than as *owner*. However, this arrangement, too, can create problems. First, as trusts cannot marry, a trust cannot qualify for the "spousal continuation" exception of Section 72(s)(3). Moreover, a trust cannot be a "designated beneficiary" and cannot, therefore, be eligible for the "distribution over life expectancy" exception to the five year rule of IRC Section 72(s)(2). It should be noted that not everyone agrees with that last statement. Some commentators point to the fact that Section

72(s)(2)(A), in defining when the annuitization option of Section 72(s)(2)(B) is available, requires only that the holder's interest be "payable to (*or for the benefit of*) [emphasis added] a designated beneficiary". Would not a trust *acting as the agent of the trust beneficiaries* be acting "for the benefit of" those beneficiaries? Moreover, did not Congress, when it enacted Section 72(s) intend to provide "parity" between the rules governing post-death distributions from IRAs and qualified plans and the rules governing such distributions from non-qualified annuities? The legislative history of 72(s) certainly suggests as much. Perhaps for those reasons, a few insurers allow the payout of a deferred annuity of which a trust is named beneficiary to be taken over a period not exceeding the life expectancy of the oldest trust beneficiary. Most insurers do not, and require distribution of the entire value of the annuity within five years, probably because, while the "parity" argument is persuasive (especially, as the IRS has accepted the validity of "look through" trusts in its application of the Required Minimum Distribution rules of IRC Sect. 401(a)(9)), there is as yet no *statutory* authority for it.

When a deferred annuity is purchased by a "special needs trust"

A deferred annuity is sometimes recommended as an investment for a "Special Needs Trust". This may be a suitable recommendation for several tax and non-tax reasons. If the trust qualifies as the "agent of a natural person", the annuity would enjoy tax-deferral; given the compressed tax rates to which trusts are often subject, such deferral may be a significant advantage. However, it may be that the interest of the state in which the trust is established, to the extent of required "paybacks" by the trust of Medicaid benefits made to the trust beneficiary, could be held to constitute a beneficiary's interest, such that the trust may not qualify as the "agent of a natural person", causing annual gains in the annuity to be taxable as earned.

When a deferred annuity is owned by a QTIP trust

As Gary Underwood observes[4], a deferred annuity may not be an appropriate investment for a QTIP trust, because undistributed gains in the annuity may not, in the laws of some states, be considered "income" and, thus, may not have to be distributed to the spouse beneficiary. The trustee could, of course, make withdrawals from the annuity and distribute them to that spouse beneficiary. However, if he or she is under the age of 59 ½, the penalty tax of Sect. 72(q) may apply. Even where that is not the case, the trustee would, in this scenario, be placed in a position of having to make such withdrawals and payments at the cost of growth of trust assets (to the detriment of the remainder beneficiaries of the trust). As Underwood notes, that may cause problems if all beneficiaries of the trust are not in agreement on the extent to which such payments of "income" should be made.

---

1 An *immediate* annuity is not subject to this rule, by the exception of IRC Sect. 72(u)(3)(E)

2 J. Gary Underwood, "Trust Ownership of Nonqualified Annuities: General Consideration for Trustees", *Journal of Financial Service Professionals,* May, 2010, footnote 45

3 Underwood, *Op cit.;* Bruce A Tannahill, "Are Nonqualified Annuities Trust-Worthy? Avoiding Tax Traps When A Trust Owns Or Is Beneficiary Of A Nonqualified Annuity", *Probate & Property,* Vol. 20, Number 4 (July-August, 2006)

4 Underwood, *Op. cit.*

Chapter 5: Suitability and Annuities

"Suitability" as a matter of *jurisdiction*

"Suitability" can be defined as "the quality of having the properties that are right for a specific purpose or situation". While that's a pretty fair general definition, the term has a more specific meaning when applied to annuity transactions, a meaning which continues to evolve as various regulatory authorities seek to pin down when an annuity transaction will or will not be considered "suitable". At the present time, there is no real precision on that point in the rulemaking of most regulatory agencies; few rules offer any *intensional* definitions (that is, specification of the necessary and sufficient conditions that must apply if a given transaction is to qualify as "suitable") or *ostensive* definitions (providing examples). Indeed, until recently, some state regulations dealing with suitability in annuity transactions were simply self-recursive (that is, they defined a suitable annuity transaction as one that is suitable). In recent years, however, regulators at both the Federal and state levels have attempted to clarify what annuity transactions (meaning, generally, sales recommendations) would be acceptable. Much of this effort was initiated by the National Association of Insurance Commissioners (NAIC) and the National Association of Securities Dealers (NASD), now known as the Financial Industry Regulatory Authority (FINRA).

The NAIC is the standards-setting and regulatory support organization created and governed by the chief insurance regulators of the 50 states, the District of Columbia, and five U.S. territories. It creates and promulgates model regulations dealing with all aspects of insurance. The NASD was founded in 1939 to supervise the conduct of its members (security dealers) subject to the oversight of the Securities and Exchange Commission (SEC). In 2007, the SEC approved the merger of the NASD and NYSE Regulation, Inc., the enforcement arm of the New York Stock Exchange, into FINRA, a private corporation that acts as a self-regulatory authority having oversight over all securities firms that do business with the U.S. public.

Chapter 5: Suitability and Annuities

The NAIC, through its member state insurance regulators, has regulatory authority over *insurance*. FINRA has authority over dealers in *securities*. Both these entities are active in developing suitability rules for annuity transactions because some - but not all - annuities are both *insurance products* and *securities*. Since 1959, *variable* annuities have been considered "securities", subject to SEC regulation[1]. They are also "insurance" and are subject to the jurisdiction of state insurance regulators. Fixed annuities, by contrast, are generally exempt from regulation as securities under Section 3(a)(8) of the Securities Act of 1933.

The status of fixed indexed annuities is less clear. In 2008, the SEC published Rule 151A which declared these contracts to be securities, subject to its jurisdiction. The rule was successfully challenged and the rule vacated[2] on a technicality; the SEC subsequently withdrew Rule 151A. While many believed, even after those events, that index annuities were still, properly speaking, "securities" (a position still held by many thoughtful observers), the issue was arguably put to rest by Sect. 989J of the Dodd-Frank financial reform act of 2010. The language of this section (often known as the "Harkin amendment" after the Senator who proposed it) was designed to keep regulation of indexed annuities with the states and not with the SEC. Interestingly, it did so by making such exemption from SEC jurisdiction contingent upon compliance with a new test of suitability.

To qualify for the Sect. 3(a)(8) exemption of the 1933 Act, any insurance or annuity contract must either –

a. [Sect. 989J(a)(3)(A)] *if issued on or after June 16, 2013,* be issued in a state (or by an insurer domiciled in a state) that has adopted suitability rules governing sale of such policies that substantially meet or exceed the minimum requirements of the NAIC Suitability in Annuity Transactions Model Reg #275, adopted in March, 2010 (SATMR) *and "any further successions thereto"* within 5 years of the NAIC's adoption of such successors *or*

b. be issued by an insurer that has adopted and implemented sales practices on a nationwide scale that substantially meet or exceed those same minimum requirements (including the "successors thereto" provision). This condition (Sect. 989J(a)(3)(B)) does not specify a date by which it must be met, which *could* mean that only way in which such an insurance or annuity contract issued prior to 6/16/13 can meet the suitability requirements of Sect. 989J would be if *the issuing insurer* had adopted and implemented sales practices meeting those requirements prior to such issue - *even if the state in which the contract is issued had already adopted suitability rules satisfying those same requirements*[3].

There are many uncertainties connected with Sect. 989J, including –

- Must the insurance comply with SATMR for all its products, or only the products seeking to rely on the "safe harbor" of Sect. 989J?
- Must all elements of SATMR be met in *all* states in which the product is offered, even in those states that have not adopted that Model Regulation[4]?

These questions and others await clarification from the SEC. For the advisor who recommends or gives advice about annuities, however, no clarification is needed; compliance with the suitability rules of SATMR is clearly the best course of action for at least two reasons: First, because many states have already adopted rules at least as stringent as those of SATMR and it's a very safe bet that all states will do so within a fairly short time. Second, because it's both ethically and practically the right thing to do.

According to an unofficial statement of the chair and vice chair of the Life Insurance and Annuities Committee of the NAIC, the Suitability in Annuity Transactions Model Regulation, was adopted by the NAIC in March, 2010 to -

Chapter 5: Suitability and Annuities

1. Establish a regulatory framework that holds insurers responsible for ensuring that annuity transactions are suitable, even if the insurer contracts with an outside party to supervise or monitor the recommendations made in the marketing and sales of annuities.

2. Require that producers be trained on the provisions of annuities in general, and the specific products they are selling.

3. Where feasible and rational, to make these suitability standards consistent with the suitability standards imposed by the Financial Industry Regulatory Authority (FINRA)[5].

That third sentence makes clear that the NAIC, while it is an organization responsible for developing and adopting rules relating to the sale and marketing of annuity products, is not the *only* entity with this responsibility and authority. FINRA, a creature of the SEC, is tasked with such duty with respect to annuities that are *securities*. As noted above, variable annuities fall into this category.

In short, the marketing of annuities is subject to regulation by multiple jurisdictions – state insurance departments, the NAIC indirectly (to the extent that the insurance regulations of the states having authority over a particular annuity sale reflect NAIC Model Regulations), and, if the annuity is a security, FINRA and the SEC. The language of the regulations issued by these different authorities is often similar or even identical (e.g.: the "suitability factors" listed in SATMR are precisely those enumerated in FINRA's Rule 2330, originally published in NASD Rule 2821). However, the rules are not always the same.

Examples:
1. As of October, 2011, twenty one states have adopted in their annuity regulations mandatory annuity training requirements, but some states require only four hours of training (the minimum number required by SATMR), while California requires eight hours.

2. Some states require ongoing annuity training; others do not.
3. Some states require *product specific* training; others do not.

While nothing prevents a state from adopting rules *in addition to* or *more stringent than* those required by SATMR, the requirements of that Model Regulation *and any NAIC Model Regulations adopted to succeed it* are now, and will continue to be, *minimum standards*. No state may adopt *less* stringent rules unless it wishes to risk having annuity contracts issued within its borders fail to qualify as "exempt securities" because the incorporation in Section 989J of Dodd-Frank of the SATMR requirements amounts to a "supremacy clause"[6].

Let's look now at the provisions of SATMR – the NAIC Suitability in Annuity Transactions Model Regulation #275 (adopted March, 2010).

SATMR: When is a recommendation regarding an annuity "suitable"?

Section 6A of the Model Regulation, entitled "Duties of Insurers and of Insurance Producers" provides a general four part test of suitability. It states –

A. In recommending to a consumer the purchase of an annuity or the exchange of an annuity that results in another insurance transaction or series of insurance transactions, the insurance producer, or the insurer where no producer is involved, shall have reasonable grounds for believing that the recommendation is suitable for the consumer on the basis of facts disclosed by the consumer as to his or her investments and other insurance products and as to his or her financial situation and needs, including the consumer's suitability information, and that there is reasonable basis to believe all of the following:

(1) The consumer has been reasonably informed of various features of the annuity, such as the potential surrender period and surrender charge, potential tax penalty if the consumer sells, exchanges, surrenders or annuitizes the annuity, mortality and expense fees, investment advisory fees,

potential charges for and features of riders, limitations on interest returns, insurance and investment components and market risk;

(2) The consumer would benefit from certain features of the annuity, such as tax-deferred growth, annuitization or death or living benefit;

(3) The particular annuity as a whole, the underlying subaccounts to which funds are allocated at the time of purchase or exchange of the annuity, and riders and similar product enhancements, if any, are suitable (and in the case of an exchange or replacement, the transaction as a whole is suitable) for the particular consumer based on his or her suitability information; and

(4) In the case of an exchange or replacement of an annuity, the exchange or replacement is suitable including taking into consideration whether:

(a) The consumer will incur a surrender charge, be subject to the commencement of a new surrender period, lose existing benefits (such as death, living or other contractual benefits), or be subject to increased fees, investment advisory fees or charges for riders and similar product enhancements;

(b) The consumer would benefit from product enhancements and improvements; and

(c) The consumer has had another annuity exchange or replacement and, in particular, an exchange or replacement within the preceding 36 months.

This four part test is a considerable improvement in specificity over previous regulations. But the Model Regulation goes further in specifying, in Section 5I, the information that an insurance producer or insurer should consider in making a determination of suitability. It defines "suitability information" as "information that is reasonably appropriate to determine the suitability of a recommendation, including the following:

1. Age
2. Annual income

3. Financial situation and needs, including the financial resources used for the funding of the annuity
4. Financial experience
5. Financial objectives
6. Intended use of the annuity
7. Financial time horizon
8. Existing assets, including investment and life insurance holdings
9. Liquidity needs
10. Liquid net worth
11. Risk tolerance
12. Tax status

These twelve factors and much of the language in this NAIC Model Regulation are taken from NASD Rule 2821 (now FINRA Rule 2330), originally published in NASD Reg. Notice 09-32 (June, 2009). This duplication of language is common in insurance regulation, where one agency, in order to be consistent with or in compliance with another agency's earlier regulation, will use similar or identical wording.

While SATMR represents a considerable improvement over previous guidance on the issue of suitability (as represented by the statutes of most states as of 2010 and by earlier NAIC Model Regulations), it does *not* provide either the acknowledgment of producer discretion or of the rebuttable presumption of suitability that had been included in the draft of an earlier NAIC model regulation (that was never adopted). That proposed NAIC Life Insurance and Annuity Model Regulation of 2002 included the following guidance, in Sect. 6 (Duties of Insurance Producers): *Insurance producers shall have reasonable discretion...to determine what information is relevant or necessary for any specific insurance transaction.*

Section 7 (Compliance) of that Model Regulation declared that "*a rebuttable presumption that a recommendation was suitable recommendation is created if the insurer or insurance producer can demonstrate:*
(1) Collection and consideration of relevant information;
(2) Conformance with an insurer's guidelines and procedures, prior to making a recommendation; and

(3) That the insurance transaction assisted the consumer in meeting the consumer's insurable needs or financial objectives.

Presumably, the recitation of twelve factors to be considered in a determination of suitability supplants the "reasonable discretion" granted in that earlier draft regulation, but one is left to wonder if the NAIC considers that a recommendation made by an advisor who took into account all those twelve factors would be *presumed* (rebuttably) to be "suitable". SATMR does not tell us.

FINRA: When is a recommendation regarding an annuity "suitable"?

As was observed earlier, the NAIC is not the only regulatory authority that may make rules regarding annuity sales. State insurance departments have that duty and many of the regulations they impose are adaptations or adoptions of NAIC models. Moreover, FINRA (and, before FINRA, the NASD) and the SEC have jurisdiction over *variable* annuities because those contracts are *securities.*. Various rules come into play when the issue is whether an annuity recommendation is "suitable".

FINRA Rule 2390

This "Know Your Customer" rule applies to all securities sales. FINRA Rule 2390, announced in FINRA's Regulatory Notice 11-02 in January, 2010, is modeled after NYSE Rule 405(1). It requires FINRA member firms to use "reasonable diligence" and to know the "essential facts" concerning their customers. According to the Regulatory Notice, *"The rule explains that "essential facts" are "those required to (a) effectively service the customer's account, (b) act in accordance with any special handling instructions for the account, (c) understand the authority of each person acting on behalf of the customer and (d) comply with applicable laws, regulations, and rules." The know-your-customer obligation arises at the beginning of the customer-broker relationship and does not depend on whether the broker has made a recommendation"*.

FINRA Rule 2111

This *suitability* rule is modeled after NASD Rule 2310 and applies to recommendations of any security. It requires that the investment firm or its "associated person" (read: "registered representative") have a reasonable basis to believe that a recommended transaction *or investment strategy* involving a security is suitable for the customer, based upon *"the information obtained through the reasonable diligence of the [FINRA] member or associated person [registered representative] to ascertain the customer's investment profile"*[7].

"Investment profile" investment profile *"includes, but is not limited to, the customer's age, other investments, financial situation and needs, tax status, investment objectives, investment experience, investment time horizon, liquidity needs, risk tolerance, and any other information the customer may disclose to the member or associated person in connection with such recommendation"*[8].

Rule 2211 explicitly applies to recommended investment strategies involving a security and is triggered when a security or strategy is recommended regardless of whether the transaction results in a transaction[9].

FINRA Rule 2330

This FINRA *annuity suitability* rule, modeled after NASD Rule 2821, applies "to recommended purchases and exchanges of deferred variable annuities and recommended initial subaccount allocations"[10]. It declares that –

No member or person associated with a member shall recommend to any customer the purchase or exchange of a deferred variable annuity unless such member or person associated with a member has a reasonable basis to believe -

(A) that the transaction is suitable in accordance with NASD Rule 2310 and, in particular, that there is a reasonable basis to believe that -
(i) the customer has been informed, in general terms, of various features of deferred variable annuities, such as the potential surrender period and surrender charge; potential tax penalty if customers sell or redeem deferred variable annuities before reaching the age of 59½;

85

mortality and expense fees; investment advisory fees; potential charges for and features of riders; the insurance and investment components of deferred variable annuities; and market risk;

(ii) the customer would benefit from certain features of deferred variable annuities, such as tax-deferred growth, annuitization, or a death or living benefit; and

(iii) the particular deferred variable annuity as a whole, the underlying subaccounts to which funds are allocated at the time of the purchase or exchange of the deferred variable annuity, and riders and similar product enhancements, if any, are suitable (and, in the case of an exchange, the transaction as a whole also is suitable) for the particular customer based on the information required by paragraph (b)(2) of this Rule; and

(B) in the case of an exchange of a deferred variable annuity, the exchange also is consistent with the suitability determination required by paragraph (b)(1)(A) of this Rule, taking into consideration whether -

(i) the customer would incur a surrender charge, be subject to commencement of a new surrender period, lose existing benefits (such as death, living, or other contractual benefits), or be subject to increased fees or charges (such as mortality and expense fees, investment advisory fees, or charges for riders and similar product enhancements);

(ii) the customer would benefit from product enhancements and improvements; and

(iii) the customer has had another deferred variable annuity exchange within the preceding 36 months[11].

Sect. B(2) of Rule 2330 lists the factors that should be considered before the recommendation of an annuity. It declares that

"Prior to recommending the purchase or exchange of a deferred variable annuity, a member or person associated with a member shall make reasonable efforts to obtain, at a minimum, information concerning the customer's age, annual income, financial situation and needs, investment experience, investment objectives, intended use of the deferred variable annuity, investment time horizon, existing assets (including investment and life insurance holdings), liquidity needs, liquid net worth, risk tolerance, tax status, and such other information used or considered to be reasonable by the member or person associated with the member in making recommendations to customers".

These are the same 12 factors cited in NASD Rule 2821 and in the NAIC's SATMR. The scope of these rules, however, is very different. The FINRA rule applies only to *variable* annuities, which are *securities*. The NAIC rule, however, applies to the sale of *any* annuity, and because the provisions of that rule have been incorporated into Section 989J of Dodd-Frank, which establishes suitability rules for the sale of "any insurance or endowment policy or annuity contract or optional annuity contract", the suitability governing the sale of *variable* annuities are now (or will be, by June 16, 2013) expanded to cover the sale of *any* annuity contract by *any* agent (whether or not securities registered).[12]

As we have seen, the question of when an annuity recommendation is "suitable" can be answered only by reference to the rules of the various agencies having jurisdiction of that recommendation, specifically and *always* including the rules of the insurance department of each state having jurisdiction over that recommendation. But this question of "suitability" is not only a matter of jurisdiction, but also of the *standard of care* that is applicable to the person making the recommendation.

"Suitability" as a matter of "Standard of Care"

At the present time, there are two standards of care in the financial services industry. The *suitability* standard applies to insurance agents and registered representatives (referred to in Dodd-Frank and some other regulatory documents as "brokers"). It requires, as we've seen, that anyone recommending an annuity reasonably believe that it is *suitable* for the client, given the client's situation and goals (and in light of the factors that must be taken into account under applicable rules).

A higher standard, applicable to *investment advisors*[13], is "fiduciary duty". Unlike the "suitability" standard, which is "rules-based", the fiduciary standard is "principles-based" and eludes a precise definition. Indeed, David Tittsworth, Executive Director of the Investment Adviser Association observes that the lack of a strict definition of "fiduciary" "is part of the reason that it works"[14]. That said, there are key elements that are generally accepted to be indispensible to the fiduciary duty. They include –

- o The duty to act in the best interest of the client
- o The duty to respect the confidentiality of client information
- o The duty to make full disclosure of all material facts about the advisory relationship, including all conflicts of interest
- o The duty to act competently

As of October, 2011, the fiduciary standard generally does not apply to insurance agents or brokers when rendering advice that is "solely incidental to the conduct of his business as a broker or dealer and who receives no special compensation therefore"[15]. However, given the current strong demand – by many consumer advocates, regulators, members of Congress, and many financial services professionals – for a "harmonization" of the two standards of care (*suitability* and *fiduciary*) or a *unified* fiduciary standard that would apply to *all* advisors, it may be that future recommendations of annuities, when made by someone now subject only to the *suitability* standard, will be scrutinized under a more exacting lens.

Let's apply such a lens now to the twelve factors which SATMR and Sect. 989J of Dodd-Frank oblige an advisor to consider before making a recommendation[16].

1. Age.

The proposed annuity buyer's age is one of the most important factors in determining the suitability of an annuity. One question that should be raised immediately is *whose age?* Will the buyer of the annuity (the proposed owner) also be the annuitant? If not, problems can result (see Chapter 2). Often, the annuitant and owner are not the same individual because the insurer will not issue an annuity where the *annuitant* is over a certain age. To avoid losing the sale, some agents will name the buyer as owner and a younger relative as *annuitant,* not realizing the implications of such a decision.

Even where the annuitant and owner are the same individual, age is an issue that is key to the suitability of the annuity. Many regulatory authorities have increased their scrutiny of annuity sales to senior citizens. The NAIC and insurance regulators in many states have issued "Consumer Alerts", warning seniors of "deceptive sales practices. Some states impose special restrictions upon the provisions that annuities sold to seniors may contain (e.g.: a maximum term and/or initial amount of surrender charges).

The suitability of certain riders, such as guaranteed death benefit and guaranteed living benefits, is also highly sensitive to age.

2. Annual Income

The annual income of the applicant for an annuity is a factor that should be considered (and, certainly, known) by the agent recommending that annuity. If the annuity is a "flexible premium" contract and ongoing contributions (premiums) are contemplated, the question of whether the applicant can afford to make those ongoing contributions is clearly relevant. If the annuity is of the "single premium" type, client income is still relevant, especially if there is any expectation that distributions from the annuity may be required to augment that income.

3. Financial Situation And Needs, Including The Financial Resources Used For The Funding Of The Annuity

If the annuity is a tool to meet financial needs, the nature and extent of those needs must be known in advance. Moreover, the source of funds is of vital importance, not only because it's a part of the client's "total picture", but also because it must be ascertained before the agent can be sure that he or she holds the licenses and registrations required by the regulators of the state in which the sale is made. If an agent recommends that a consumer sell holdings that are *securities* and use the proceeds to purchase an annuity, that agent must be registered, either as an investment advisor or as a registered representative entitled to give advice about the type of securities recommended to be sold.

Example: Joe Advisor recommends that a deferred annuity would be more suitable for Cathy Consumer than the mutual funds she now owns. Joe would need to hold a "Series 6" registration ("Investment Company Products/Variable Contracts Limited Representative") to give such advice. If Cathy's holdings were common stocks or bonds, Joe would need a "Series 7" registration ("General Securities Representative"). This is true even if the annuity Joe recommends is not a variable contract. Of course, if it is, Joe would need at least a "Series 6" to make such a recommendation, regardless of "source of funds".

There is a widespread misperception that if the "source of funds" includes securities, the agent recommending an annuity must *always* possess a securities registration (or be a registered investment advisor). Often, those who believe this to be true will cite state regulations such as the *Joint Bulletin No. 14-2009* issued by the Arkansas Insurance and Securities departments in September, 2009, which stated –

> *"The recommendation to replace securities such as mutual funds, stocks, bonds and various other investment vehicles defined as securities under the Arkansas Securities Act is the offering of investment advice. It is unlawful to offer investment advice unless one is registered (licensed) with the Arkansas Securities Department as an investment adviser or investment adviser representative."*

But that text does not say that the proceeds of the sale of securities may never be used to purchase an annuity unless the agent recommending that annuity is securities registered. It says only that the agent may not *recommend* such liquidation without being registered *as an investment advisor (or investment advisor representative)*. Clearly, a Series 6 or Series 7 registration would not suffice in Arkansas because the regulators in that state have defined a recommendation to replace securities as the rendering of "investment advice". In another state, such a recommendation may be considered to fall within the "solely incidental" exception of Sect. 202(a)(11)(C) of the Investment Advisers Act of 1940 (see p. 86. *supra*).

Generally, however, an agent who recommends a non-variable annuity will not be obliged to be securities registered even if the source of funds is securities *provided that he or she does not actually recommend the replacement of those securities*. But how safe is this harbor? Can a non-registered agent recommending an annuity that is purchased with funds resulting from the sale of purchaser's securities reasonably claim "I did not know that's where the money came from"? A strict reading of this suitability provision ("3. Financial Situation And Needs, Including The Financial Resources Used For The Funding Of The Annuity") would, in the author's opinion, not support such a plea, absent clear evidence that the consumer told the agent that the annuity funding would come from other sources.

It is vitally important that anyone recommending an annuity to a purchaser know what funds will be used to fund that annuity and the registration implications of that knowledge.

4. Financial experience

The financial experience of the client is arguably more important if the annuity being recommended is a variable or indexed product than if it's a conventional fixed annuity, because the former products are far more complicated. Moreover, if the annuity is a variable one, the familiarity of the client with the types of investments offered in the separate accounts is essential. But it is at least arguable that ascertaining – and documenting - the financial experience – and financial sophistication – of the client is no less important when an index annuity is being considered.

5. Financial objectives

This one comes down to "what are we trying to accomplish with this annuity?" If the annuity is the tool, the financial objectives are the jobs to be done. The more everyone understands the nature of those jobs, the better they can ascertain whether the annuity in question is the right tool. "Everyone" here, means not only the applicant and agent, but also the insurance company - and, arguably at least, the beneficiaries – especially if the applicant is of an advanced age. Putting the beneficiaries of a senior citizen client in the information loop, up front, can greatly reduce the risks of misunderstanding (and, possibly, litigation) later on.

6. Intended use of the annuity

Here, again, we're talking about the "tool" and the "job". The appropriateness of any annuity is hugely dependent upon the job it's intended to do. Is the annuity expected to serve as an accumulation instrument? As a source of income? As a mechanism for deferring income taxes? Is creditor protection an issue? Is providing a legacy for heirs a major concern? (If that's a major intended use, has life insurance been considered?) A detailed discussion of this subject ("what are you going to do with this money?") will enhance client confidence in the agent, increase client satisfaction with the purchase, and go a long way towards eliminating future misunderstandings.

7. Financial time horizon

"Time horizon" can be a confusing term. It might mean the maximum period during which this investment will be held. Or it might mean the number of years before which distributions (income) will be needed. The author has seen it used both ways. Both are relevant to a determination of suitability, and the author suggests that both should be discussed, and the client's estimates for both be documented.

8. Existing assets, including investment and life insurance holdings

Why are the annuity applicant's other assets of relevance to the suitability of the annuity being proposed? For several reasons. First, because the type and total value of those other assets shed light on the extent to which the financial objectives identified in concern #5, above are likely to be met. Second, they serve as a "check" on the applicant's responses in several of the other concerns. For example, if this applicant claims substantial financial experience (concern #4), little need for liquidity (concern #9), a high tolerance for market risk (concern #11), and a high marginal tax bracket, yet all, or nearly all, of his existing assets are certificates of deposit and money market accounts, a discussion of how the risk and reward characteristics of a savings or investment product (such as an annuity) can "match up" with the investor's goals and concerns is probably in order.

9. Liquidity Needs

The "liquidity" of an asset refers to how quickly and cheaply it can be converted to cash. While a deferred annuity that imposes surrender charges (as most do) can be surrendered for cash relatively quickly, the cash received might, because of those charges, be significantly less than the annuity's value just prior to surrender. In a few index annuities, surrender charges never expire, and may even apply to death proceeds taken in a lump sum; those annuities may be considered relatively "illiquid". But even those contracts whose charges do expire after a term of years may have a high cost for early liquidity during that surrender charge period.

10. Liquid Net Worth

If liquidity is a concern that must be addressed on every annuity sale (and it is), liquid net worth is a vitally important factor, because it's the value of the applicant's assets that are liquid – that can be converted to cash quickly and cheaply. If Mr. Jones has, say, $100,000 in a money market account (which is highly liquid) and his financial objectives, time horizon, and liquidity need are such that the $100,000 will almost certainly not be required while surrender charges of the proposed annuity apply, liquidity, for the money to be invested in the annuity may not be of great concern – so long as that $100,000 will remain liquid after the annuity sale.

A Note About "Liquidity" and Annuity Surrender Charges

A determination of whether a deferred annuity is or is not "suitable" under a particular set of facts often includes a consideration of the surrender charges imposed by that contract. (*See Chapter 1 for a detailed explanation of surrender charges*). Indeed, in the

Chapter 5: Suitability and Annuities

author's experience (which includes nearly forty years service as an insurance agent and over a decade as an expert witness in litigation involving annuities), surrender charges are nearly always an element in such a reckoning.

Complaints to regulators or lawsuits involving annuity sales typically allege that the buyer did not fully understand either the amount of surrender charges or the conditions under which they would be imposed. While these charges are always set forth in the annuity contract, not all contracts explain them in simple language; moreover, the conditions under which the charges will be waived are often not clear at all. "Point of Sale" brochures are often little better in this regard. How might an advisor improve the chances that a buyer truly understands surrender charges – or that he or she can demonstrate to regulators, arbitrators, or a jury that they were fully explained? The author suggests, in workshops he conducts for agents, a few techniques:

- If the annuity is a variable one, where a prospectus must be delivered to the purchaser at the time of application, the advisor should review the section(s) in the prospectus dealing with surrender charges. If the annuity is not variable, the advisor should review with the purchaser a specimen contract of the annuity being recommended. In both cases, the advisor should make a note of this activity in the client's file. Sadly, many advisors the author has spoken with have never even seen a specimen contract.

- Most, if not all, issuers of annuities now require "Suitability Questionnaires" to be submitted with the annuity application. These documents typically disclose charges and, often, require the purchaser to acknowledge (by signature or initials) that those charges were explained. This is an excellent practice that should be universally followed.

- When reviewing "point of sale" material such as product brochures, the advisor should ask the purchaser to initial or sign the brochure alongside the description of surrender charges on both the copy given to the client and the copy retained by the advisor in the client's file.

- The advisor should review with the purchaser why surrender charges exist. As explained in Chapter 1, they are not wholly a "drawback" of deferred annuities; rather, they allow an insurer to credit a competitive rate of interest (or other earnings) to the policy owner without risk of loss due to early surrenders.

- In the author's view, most annuity complaints involving surrender charges could be avoided if the advisor asks a simple question during the sales interview: "Is there *any chance at all* that you'll need access to the funds you're considering putting into this annuity during the next N years (where N = the surrender charge period), *given the fact that you have access to the other liquid funds you've told me about?* If the answer is "yes", the advisor should *not* recommend funding the annuity with the amount originally contemplated, but recommend that *a portion* of that money be allocated to a liquid account (e.g.: a money market, checking, or savings account). That done, the process should be repeated - and again, if necessary - until the purchaser's response is "no". At that point, the advisor could ask "So you're telling me that you're comfortable *locking up* this amount of money in this annuity for N years in order to obtain the benefits we've discussed?"

Some advisors might object that this technique ignores the fact that most deferred annuities permit penalty-free withdrawals of up to a certain amount of percentage of the annuity value during the surrender charge period *and* withdrawals in excess of those amounts under certain conditions (such as nursing home confinement). That is true. But can a purchaser, told of a 10% "free withdrawal" privilege be sure that he or she might not need, say, 15%? In the author's opinion, *beginning* the discussion of surrender charges by verifying that the purchaser has liquid funds sufficient to pay for emergencies or unexpected expenses during the entire surrender charge period, and then, *and only then,* reviewing the "free withdrawal" provisions will go a long way toward ensuring that the annuity is suitable *from a "liquidity" perspective.*

11. Risk Tolerance

"Risk tolerance" is a concept absolutely vital to any determination of whether an annuity sale is (or is not) "suitable" because annuities are risk management instruments. Unfortunately, this simple fact is not widely – or well – understood by many financial advisors (or, sad to say, regulators). Moreover, the very notion of "risk" is largely misunderstood or misapplied.

What is "risk"? Textbooks in Finance tell us that there are many different kids of "risk", including market risk, interest rate risk, inflation risk, currency risk, credit risk, liquidity risk, etc. Yet many "risk tolerance questionnaires" used by financial advisors (and often required by insurers and/or broker/dealers to be completed prior to the sale of an annuity – especially a variable annuity) focus only on one of these – market risk, which is commonly defined in either of two very different ways.

One definition says that "market risk" is "the risk that market pressures may cause the value of an investment to fluctuate". In that sense, "market risk" means "volatility". Another, equally widely-held, says that "market risk" is the possibility that market pressures will cause the value of an investment to decline. In that sense, "market risk" equals "principal risk". Both involve uncertainty (which, we believe, is the central element of "risk") as to the future value of one's capital.

Certainly, that's an important consideration to any investor; but it's not all-important. The widespread use of risk tolerance assessment tool (such as a questionnaire) that identifies "risk" only as the possibility of losing one's capital (or principal) focuses attention only on the "capital preservation" and "wealth accumulation" potential of the product being considered (concerning which the tool is employed).

Why can that be a problem when such a tool is used to determine the suitability of an annuity? Because the risk that is of greatest concern to the investor may not be "that I might lose some *principal*", but, rather, that "I might run out of *income*". Moreover, principal risk is not really a factor when an immediate annuity is being proposed (because an immediate annuity amounts to an exchange of capital (principal) for income). And it may not be a factor when the product proposed is a fixed deferred annuity, because all fixed deferred annuities guarantee principal (except to the extent that surrender charges or a market value adjustment may erode principal if the contract is surrendered early). Indeed, principal risk may not be a great concern even when the proposed product is a variable deferred annuity if a "guaranteed living benefit" has been chosen (because the *income* guaranteed with such benefits is often immune to adverse market performance).

The author is certainly not suggesting that market risk shouldn't be a concern when one is determining the suitability of a proposed investment, but only that many "risk tolerance" measurement tools focus only on market risk — and, in doing so, marginalize, or ignore completely, the applicant's tolerance for other risks that may be of far greater concern. The author believes that any discussion of "risk tolerance" should be informed by the applicant's responses to the other eleven factors identified in that Regulation — especially, financial objectives, intended use of the annuity, financial time horizon, and liquidity needs.

12. Tax Status

An applicant's tax status is obviously important in any determination of the suitability of a proposed investment because different investments get different tax treatment, and the utility of a given tax treatment depends largely on the taxpayer's existing tax situation and on the type of account in which the investment will be held. When the investment being proposed is a deferred annuity, "tax status" acquires special significance, because deferred annuities enjoy tax deferred growth.

A Final Note

The issue of "suitability", as it applies to the recommendation of annuity products, is a complex one; not only are "the rules" not entirely consistent from one jurisdiction to another, but the rules of the individual jurisdiction are in almost constant revision, though a few elements will persist.

- The suitability of a particular annuity in a particular situation will always be a matter of facts and circumstances. That said, if the factors cited in SATMR are properly considered by the agent/advisor before recommending an annuity, unsuitability should be minimized, and egregiously unsuitable sales could become a rarity.

- The present "suitability" standard is almost certain to become more stringent. The current push for "harmonization" of the two standard of care regimes or for a *single fiduciary standard* applying to all those who give financial advice will, in the author's opinion, inevitably produce a standard of care for annuity advisors incorporating elements now confined to the fiduciary standard. Disclosure of commissions will, he believes, become obligatory, *which should not adversely affect those advisors who are already employing the kind of diligent suitability practices that the regulations we've examined seek to mandate.*

- For those advisors who are subject to more than one standard of care (e.g.: registered representatives who are also registered investment advisors or advisory associates), it is possible, if not likely, that they will be held to the highest standard that would apply to them, regardless of the "type of case". In other words, a broker who, when selling a fixed annuity is currently held only to the standard of *suitability* may, if he is also an investment advisor (or associate), be held in future to the *fiduciary* standard applicable when he acts as an investment advisor - even when he is "merely selling product". Broker/Dealers are unlikely to be willing to guess, when overseeing the activities of their representatives, which hat those representatives are wearing in any given interaction with consumers.

- Education requirements will continue to stiffen. SATMR requires any agent who sells any annuity to complete at least a four-hour course on annuities. Many Broker/Dealers and insurers also require such training. Given the growing complexity of annuity products and a litigious consumer population, increased competency is both ethically laudable and very good business.

---

1 *S.E.C. v. Variable Annuity Life Insurance Co.*, 359 U.S. 65 (1959)

2 *American Equity Investment Life Insurance Co. v. S.E.C. 2009 WL 2152351* (D.C. Cir. July 21, 2009).

3 As the "safe harbor" language in Sect. 989J(a)(3)(A) - providing that such a contract will be deemed an exempt security if the issuing state has adopted suitability rules consistent with SATMR (and its successors) - refers only to contracts issued on or after 6/16/13, it is arguable that contracts issued earlier cannot claim its protection.

Chapter 5: Suitability and Annuities

4 Adapted from an outline on Sect. 989J written by Mel Warshaw, J.D, with permission of the author.

5 "Suitability In Annuity Transactions Model Regulation: Regulatory Guidance" (*www.naic.org/documents/committees_a_suitability_reg_guidance.pdf*)

6 The constitutionality of a mere Federal statute invoking such Federal supremacy is both beyond the scope of this book and the expertise of its author. That said, the author finds it interesting, at least, that, at a time when insurance regulation is generally conceded to be the province of *state* insurance commissioners, a Federal statute can declare that unless those commissioners adopt rules promulgated by their own association within a time not of their own choosing, insurance products that they have the duty to regulate will be deemed to be within the jurisdiction of a Federal agency tasked only with the regulation of *securities*.

7 FINRA Regulatory Notice 11-02, January 2011

8 Ibid

9 Ibid

10 FINRA Regulatory Notice 10-05, January 2010

11 The quoted text (from FINRA Rule 2330(b)) is identical to the language in NASD Rule 2821(b).

12 The extent to which 989J also mandates suitability rules for insurance products other than annuities is beyond the scope of this book.

13 Defined in Sect. 202(a)(11) of the Investment Advisers Act of 1940 as "any person who, for compensation, engages in the business of advising others, either directly or through publications or writings, as to the value of securities or as to the advisability of investing in, purchasing, or selling securities, or who, for compensation and as part of a regular business, issues or promulgates analyses or reports concerning securities".

14 Quoted in Julie DiMauro, "The Elusive Fiduciary Definition" (Complinet, Sept, 2009 - www.liftburden.com/Complinet%200909%20Fiduciary.pdf)

15 Investment Advisers Act of 1940, Sect. 202(a)(11)(C)

16 The following discussion of the SATMR "12 factors" is adapted from Index Annuities: A Suitable Approach (Olsen & Marrion LLC, 2010), by permission

The following article, which appeared in the November, 2006 issue of *The Journal of Financial Service Professionals*, won First Place in the Kenneth Black, Jr. Journal Author Award for 2006.
It appears here by permission.

Annuities and Suitability: Reflections on the State of the Debate
by John L. Olsen, CLU, ChFC, AEP

ABSTRACT:
The current debate about annuities – if and when they are appropriate – is cluttered with assumptions and pre-conceptions. The polemic on both sides often obscures more than it reveals, and makes it difficult for objective advisors to judge when an annuity is or is not suitable for a client. This article examines the issues of suitability from a non-partisan position and offers some "bright line tests" as to when annuities may, or may not be, appropriate.

OVERVIEW

One of the most controversial subjects in the financial services industry these days is that of *annuities*. A great deal is being written and said about these contracts and much of it is highly favorable or highly unfavorable, often to the point of polemic. Sadly, this sort of polarized debate does little to increase understanding. Even worse, for the state of our understanding, is the fact that much of the discussion about the value, appropriateness, or suitability of annuities, even whn written from a balanced perspective, treats the subject as if it were homogenous – as if all annuities were alike, or at least so similar that one can properly make generalizations that apply to all of them.

That is simply not true; annuities are not homogenous. There are different types of annuities, and the various types are structured, and perform, *very* differently. Any assessment of the value of an annuity in a given set of facts and circumstances must specify the sort of annuity being considered. A generalization such as "an annuity is not appropriate for anyone over age 65" is simply nonsense – *not*

Annuities and Suitability: Reflections on the State of the Debate

because a valid case cannot made for the inappropriateness of *certain types* of annuities for such buyers, but because the various types are so different that the *reasons* that could reasonably be offered to support such an assessment could be valid for one type of annuity, yet totally irrelevant to another. For example, the annual costs of variable deferred annuities have no counterparts in traditional fixed deferred contracts. More to the point, deferred annuities and immediate annuities are so hugely different that a true statement about one will generally be untrue of the other.

In addition to this problem of *undifferentiation* (the failure to distinguish between the very different types of contracts when making generalizations about annuities), there is the troublesome fact that most critics of annuities, and many who favor them, frame their arguments from the perception of an annuity as an *investment*[1] vehicle. The trouble here is not that an annuity cannot be an investment, but, rather, that it's never *only* an investment. Any annuity is, to some extent, a *risk management tool*, and to the extent that it is being used as such, the charges for the risk management benefits it offers are *insurance costs*, not merely drags on investment performance. Focusing on one element of a subject, as if were the only one, is not sound analysis, and treating some costs as mere "overhead" (by dismissing, or ignoring entirely, the benefits purchased by those costs) is downright specious. Equally flawed is the focus of many proponents of deferred annuities upon the tax-deferral enjoyed by such contracts as though such treatment is always desirable and, all too often, without any consideration of the inescapable tax trade-off (the unavailability of Capital Gains treatment).

The debate over annuities would be greatly improved, and far more productive, if participants would recognize a few essential, often unconsidered, facts about these contracts. The author suggests the following for the reader's consideration (realizing that it is not a complete list):

ITEMS TO CONSIDER, WHEN DISCUSSING ANNUITIES

1. *Deferred* annuities and *immediate* annuities are very different instruments, designed to accomplish very different – indeed, mutually exclusive – objectives.

2. *Fixed* deferred annuities and *variable* deferred annuities have at least as many differences as similarities. Arguably, the defining element of each is absent in the other.

3. There is more variation, even within one specific type of annuity, than is usually acknowledged. For example, the criticism of a fixed immediate annuity as offering no inflation protection is true of only *some* contracts.

4. *Deferred* annuities are not purely *accumulation* instruments. Some types work better in that capacity than others, and all can be (and sometimes are) marketed that way, but the guarantee of a *certain* income is a central promise of every deferred annuity. (Immediate annuities, of course, are *not* accumulation tools; they're all about immediate *income*).

5. Annuities – arguably, *all* annuities – are both *investment* and *risk management* tools[2]. The guarantees they provide reduce the purchaser's risk. The cost of those guarantees may properly be considered as mere "overhead" (as drags on investment performance) only to the extent that the guarantees are judged to have no worth (that is, that they are neither needed nor wanted). This is not to say that one is obliged to value any such provision as worth the price charged. A particular buyer may, for example, consider the *guaranteed death benefit* in a variable annuity as valuable, but overpriced. If so, the *excess* cost (the difference between the contractual charge and a charge the buyer considers "fair") could logically be viewed as mere "overhead".

6. Viewing the costs and benefits of an annuity entirely with conventional financial mathematics may produce an incomplete picture. Some of the benefits annuities offer have more to do with emotion than with financial ratios. For example, if the presence of "downside guarantees" in a variable annuity (e.g.: Guaranteed Minimum Withdrawal and/or Income Benefits) enable a highly risk-averse investor to be comfortable in allocating more of his account to *equities* than he would otherwise be willing to do, thus providing that investor with greater potential gain than a lower risk/lower return allocation could be expected to produce, the annual cost of those downside guarantees might reasonably be weighed against the expected increase in return.

SOME OBSERVATIONS ON APPROPRIATENESS OF ANNUITIES

As we have observed, an annuity – any annuity – is a tool, a device intended to accomplish a particular job. How well a particular annuity will do that, relative to how well one or more specified alternatives would, depends upon (a) the job and (b) the specific type of annuity being considered. While sweeping generalizations should be avoided, it is possible to make some general observations about when annuities generally perform well and when they do not. Indeed, in the author's opinion, it is possible to assert a few "bright line tests" with regard to the appropriateness or inappropriateness of annuities in specific situations. In the following discussion, we'll examine some of the most common *goal situations* and how well – or poorly – annuities may work in those situations. Where a particular type of annuity is clearly suitable or unsuitable, the author will suggest suitability rules ("bright line tests") that will appear in **bold italics**.

Where The Goal Is *Immediate Income*

When *immediate income* is the primary goal, an *immediate annuity* may be appropriate, *provided that there is no requirement that principal be preserved*. As an immediate annuity consists of the amortized distribution of both earnings and principal, it is not appropriate when all, *or even some*, of the amount invested *must* remain at the end of the income period. A *deferred annuity* is not designed to produce income immediately. Indeed, many deferred annuities do not permit distributions during the first contract year. Those contracts that do permit distributions in the first year generally limit such distributions to contract gain.

If <u>any</u> principal must remain after the income has been distributed, an immediate annuity is inappropriate.

```
If income must commence within a year of
the   investment,   a   deferred   annuity   is
inappropriate.
```

Where The Income Amount Must Be As High As Possible On A Guaranteed Basis

Where the primary goal is income and where the amount of that income must be as high as possible *on a guaranteed basis*, an immediate annuity is ideal. The key word, here, is *guaranteed*. Where the income period is a fixed number of years, a *Period Certain* fixed immediate annuity will generally provide a greater amount than can be *assured* from any investment alternative because the non-annuity alternative must preserve principal. Where the income period is for the entire lifetime of the recipient *and* where no part of principal must remain at the expiry of that period *and* where the amount of each income payment must be assured in advance and be as high as possible, an immediate annuity is not only the most appropriate solution, but also the *only* solution.

This is true not only when the amount of each payment must be the same, but also when the amount of each year's payment must increase, by either a fixed percentage or by an index such as the Consumer Price index (CPI). It should be noted that not all immediate annuities offer such an increasing amount option and that very few offer increases tied to an external index such as the CPI.

Where the amount of income payments must be guaranteed in advance and where no principal must remain, an immediate annuity is the ideal solution.

Where the Goal Is Accumulation of Capital

Where the goal is capital accumulation, an immediate annuity is clearly not suitable, but a deferred annuity *may* be. If *preservation of principal* is a requirement, a fixed deferred annuity might be appropriate, but a variable one, *in the absence of a "Guaranteed Minimum AccumulationBenefit" rider*[3], is not. This is because a variable annuity, except to the extent that its cash value is invested in the "fixed account", does not offer safety of principal.

With the addition of this "rider" (or, if the purchaser is willing to consider a return of purchase payments *in installments* as a "guarantee of principal", a *Guaranteed Minimum Withdrawal Benefit ["GMWB"]*), a variable deferred annuity can serve as an instrument for capital accumulation with "safety of principal". Indeed, the GMWB provision of many contracts includes a "step up" feature that not only assures the return of the original investment (in installments), but also any contract gain accrued as of the point where the "step up" option may be exercised.

If safety of principal is not required (or if the riders described have been added), a variable annuity is certainly an instrument for capital accumulation. Whether it's the *right* instrument depends upon several factors.

Where All That Is Wanted Is Capital Accumulation

Where the goal is purely accumulation of capital, with no concern for assuring a minimum income later on or for a guaranteed minimum death benefit, a fixed deferred annuity may be appropriate, but, in the author's opinion, a variable annuity is probably not. This is because the ongoing contract charges (notably, the "Mortality and

Expense" charge) in these contracts, that pay for the *annuity payout* guarantees and the standard Minimum Death Benefit guarantee they contain, would, in this scenario, be all, or nearly all, "overhead cost". The average "M&E" cost in today's variable deferred annuities is, according to *Morningstar, Inc.*, approximately 1.2% of the account balance[4]. This is a significant amount to be paying, each year, for benefits one does not particularly want. By contrast, fixed deferred annuities contain no such contract charges. They offer the same annuity payout guarantees, however, and they charge for them. However, in the case of fixed contracts, the cost for these payout options is paid from the "interest rate spread" – the difference between what the issuing insurer earns and what it credits to contract holders.[5] This allows a *direct* comparison of the crediting rate offered by the fixed annuity with that of alternatives such as CDs.

All variable deferred annuities offer a "fixed account", and many advisors recommend allocating a portion of the client's money to them. There are two advantages to this strategy, in addition to the obvious diversification advantage. First, holding a portion of one's annuity money in a fixed account guarantees both safety of principal and a minimum interest rate with respect to that portion. Second, M&E charges and any optional "rider" charges are assessed only against the value of *separate* (non-fixed) accounts. But it should be noted that the *current* interest rate of the fixed account in many variable annuities is less than the current interest rate offered by the same insurer in its *fixed* deferred annuities. Funding a variable annuity entirely with the fixed account may be less attractive than simply buying a fixed annuity.

With regard to comparisons, it should be noted that, in variable contracts, the *net* return available to the purchaser is the *gross* rate earned by the underlying investments, less the operating costs at the "investment sub-account" level (comparable to the "expense ratio" of mutual funds), *less the contractual charges*. If one assumes (for purposes of comparison) that the gross return on a portfolio of VA sub accounts is the same as that of a comparable portfolio of mutual funds, the annuity imposes an additional level of costs, which inevitably results in a lower *net* return in the annuity.

Is this to say that this additional level of costs is *excessive*, or even *unnecessary*? If the benefits that these additional costs pay for are not desired (that is, that the investor does not value the annuity guarantees), then the answer, in the author's opinion, is "yes". Of course, not all investors consider annuity and minimum death benefit guarantees to be meaningless. For those who do, however, a "bright line test" emerges with regard to variable deferred annuities that do not include "Guaranteed Living Benefits":

Where the minimum death benefit and annuity payout guarantees are not important to the investor, a variable deferred annuity with no "guaranteed living benefits" is probably not appropriate.

But what about those investors who wish the "upside potential" of returns possible from a portfolio of *equity* (or *equity and bond*) investments, but with some "downside guarantees"? That's where the newer "Guaranteed Living Benefits", available in newer variable deferred annuity contracts, can be very attractive.

Where The Goal Is "Market-like" Returns With "Downside Guarantees"

Amounts invested in the "separate accounts" of a variable deferred annuity[6] enjoy neither safety of principal nor a guaranteed minimum return. The value of these accounts varies directly with the performance of the underlying investments chosen. The purchaser assumes the *investment risk* inherent in these accounts, in exchange for the potential *reward* associated with such holdings. Many investors want and need the *returns* possible when their money is "in the markets", but are unwilling to assume all the *risks* commensurate with that choice. To satisfy these investors, issuers of variable deferred annuities have developed optional "riders" to their contracts, the so-called *Guaranteed Living Benefits*. Currently, there are four types of Guaranteed Living Benefits:

1. *Guaranteed Minimum Income Benefit (GMIB)*
2. *Guaranteed Minimum Accumulation Benefit (GMAB)*
3. *Guaranteed Minimum Withdrawal Benefit (GMWB)*

4. *"Combination" Riders, employing features of two or more of the first three provisions.*

A thorough description of these riders is beyond the scope of this article. (An extensive discussion of these and other annuity provisions may be found in *The Annuity Advisor* (National Underwriter Co., 2005), by the author and Michael E. Kitces, MSFS, CFP®, CLU, ChFC). That said, one can make a general observation:, The essence of all Guaranteed Living Benefits (GLBs) is that they provide the purchaser with protection against "downside risk" (the possibility of *losing money*, due to poor investment performance). Each GLB operates differently, and some assure, not only a recovery of principal, but of principal and a stated minimum return.

The appeal of a variable deferred annuity containing a Guaranteed Living Benefit is simple: The purchaser gets the "upside potential" associated with the types of investments selected, with *insurance* against loss[7]. This makes for an attractive package – so attractive that it is sometimes marketed as "the best of all possible worlds", "the perfect retirement planning instrument", or the like.

That, in the author's opinion, is going altogether too far. For one thing, a variable deferred annuity where a Guaranteed Living Benefit has been elected is *expensive*. A typical deferred variable annuity with such benefit has a total *annual expense* approaching 300 basis points (3%) per year. GLBs are generally available only in fully commissionable contracts.

The most common Mortality, Expense, and Administration (ME&A) charge in such contracts is 1.4% per year. In addition, the purchase must pay the annual expenses of the investment accounts selected, which might add an additional 1%. While the cost of GLBs varies considerably, the range is roughly 25-75 bps/year (0.25% - 0.75%). The "Combination Rider" from several insurers costs 60 bps/year (0.6%). It is arguable that the insurance that these Guaranteed Living Benefits provide is not worth the price charged

Annuities and Suitability: Reflections on the State of the Debate

(and the same may be said of the "enhanced" Guaranteed *Death* Benefits in many of today's contracts).

Whether the *benefits* conferred by these provisions are worth the *price* charged is surely a matter for individual decision. Some investors will value these guarantees more highly than others. In addition (in the author's opinion, at least), the decision is not entirely a mathematical one, for two reasons:

First, because *quantifying* the risks transferred from the purchaser to the insurer by these riders is a daunting, if not impossible, task. There are many variables involved. Moreover,, the data from which one might make a determination is not available to most of us.

Second (and perhaps more important), quantification is difficult because the *benefits* conferred are not wholly financial. There is surely an *emotional* component. Will the investor *sleep better*, given such guarantees? If so, how important is that?

A test that might be useful in this regard is: *Would the investor rather have a hypothetical average return of X%, with no assurance of any minimum or of a certain future value or annual annuity payment, or that same average return, less* **YYY** *basis points per year, for the assurance of a certain future value or annual annuity payment* **if things go wrong?**

The technical reader will object that this test is hardly mathematically rigorous, and will be right in doing so. It is not. But it may help an investor in assessing his or her real *risk tolerance*.

Commissionable vs. Non-Commissionable Variable Annuities

Some variable annuities assess no surrender charges. Some of these assess M&E charges at or near the levels for "regular" commissionable VAs and pay reduced sales commissions or assess higher-than-usual M&E and pay normal sales commissions. Guaranteed living benefits are usually offered in these contracts. Others offer far lower M&E charges and pay no sales commissions.

Usually, these contracts do not offer guaranteed living benefits (or "enhanced" guaranteed death benefits).

What can we make of these facts? First, that surrender and M&E charges are the source of selling commissions. The so-called "low load"[8] contracts out there were designed to be sold directly to consumers or for recommendation by fee-compensated advisors. While some offer few investment choices[9], others feature many accounts from a variety of money managers. All, however, emphasize *low cost*.

Why don't these contracts offer guaranteed living benefits or "enhanced" death benefits (at optional extra costs)? One reason is that low cost is a market niche and that marketing low cost is much easier when your cost structure is both low and simple (with no "at additional cost" items). Another may be that the issuers' actuaries are not confident that they can price such benefits properly. Whatever the rationale(s), the result is a choice. One can buy a "basic" annuity, with low annual costs and no surrender charges, but no optional living or death benefits, or a "fully loaded" annuity, with optional "riders" and possibly more investment choices, but assessing higher annual costs and surrender charges. Of course, the consumer is not likely to get a recommendation for the former from an advisor whose income comes from commissions or for the latter from a "fee only" advisor. But this condition is not unique to annuities. It has existed since at least the emergence of "no load" mutual funds.

Where The Goal Is Income Later On

Where the goal is an income (perhaps an income for life) to commence *later on*, a deferred annuity, either fixed or variable, may be appropriate. *All* deferred annuities contain *guaranteed payout factors* that specify how much income the contract owner will receive, *regardless of future changes in life expectancy or interest rates*, per dollar of contract value placed under that payout option.

Is this a valuable guarantee? If one looks to the past, it would not seem so. To the author's knowledge, there has never been a time, in the 33 years that he has been selling insurance and annuities,

Annuities and Suitability: Reflections on the State of the Debate

when the payout factors *guaranteed* in *any* deferred annuity contract were as attractive as the payout factors then available in the *immediate annuity* marketplace. Indeed, this is the chief reason why so few deferred annuities are ever annuitized. One has always been able to "go shopping" for payout rates, and, finding an immediate annuity with better payout rates, exchange one's deferred annuity for that immediate one, in a tax-free exchange, under IRC §1035.

That said, the longevity of Americans is increasing, and at an increasing rate. Is it possible that the payout rates *guaranteed* in todays deferred annuities might be better than the *current* rates of immediate annuities decades from now, when average life expectancy may be far greater? Is that possibility worth *insuring?* Moreover, suppose that one assumes that future current rates will be more attractive than today's guaranteed ones and chooses some vehicle other than a deferred annuity to *accumulate* capital, intending to invest that accumulated capital, later, in an immediate annuity (to take advantage of those higher payout rates)? Will not the untaxed gain be taxed at that point, resulting in less money placed under the payout option?

Where an *assurance* of a *future* income stream is important, guaranteed annuity payout factors might not be seen as important. Guaranteed Living Benefits, on the other hand, very likely will be. Not only do such provisions rely on payout factors *guaranteed,* but those factors will be applied to a future account balance that is sure to be *at least as great* as the minimum specified in the benefit, *even if future investment performance is poor.* The assurances that these GLBs provide have proven very attractive to many investors. But it is very important to understand that these provisions are not designed to enhance returns, but to control loss. In fact, their annual cost reduces returns credited – which leads us to yet another "bright line test":

"Guaranteed Living Benefits" are appropriate when the investor is willing to trade a part of each year's return for guarantees against investment loss.

Where The Goal Is To Achieve Tax Benefits

One of the most exasperating aspects of the debate over the value of deferred annuities is the extent to which participants on both sides make rash assumptions about the income tax benefits they provide – or are claimed to provide.

Tax Arguments Offered By Annuity Proponents

Those who market these contracts have, for years, touted the fact that "gain" in a deferred annuity enjoys *income tax deferral*[10], often without even discussing the inescapable trade-offs of such treatment – namely, that –

1. Under current tax law, all distributions from annuities are taxed as Ordinary Income. They never qualify for Capital Gains treatment.
2. Early distributions from annuities are subject to a 10% penalty tax, to the extent of "gain", unless an exception to the penalty applies.
3. *Tax deferred* does not mean *tax free*. Not only will the owner inevitably pay tax on the contract gain, but so will the beneficiary (as "Income In Respect Of A Decedent").

Does the benefit of tax deferral outweigh these drawbacks? In the author's experience (which includes having done many analyses of this very question for consulting clients), the answer can be nothing more than "It depends". There are numerous variables involved, and the impact of each on the overall result is not the same in every fact situation. However, the author believes that a few generalizations can be made when comparing a deferred annuity to a currently taxable investment alternative:

1. The higher the investor's current – and, especially, future – tax bracket, the better a deferred annuity will perform (by comparison)[11].
2. The higher the portfolio *turnover rate* in the taxable alternative, the better the annuity will perform.

3. The higher the annual expense charge of the annuity (or, viewed another way, the lower the annual expense of the taxable alternative), the worse the annuity will perform.
4. The longer the accumulation period (from the initial investment until the investor begins receiving income), the better the annuity will perform.
5. The longer the distribution period (over which income will be received), the better the annuity will perform. In hundreds of analyses, the author found this variable to have the greatest impact on the final result (of whether the annuity or investment alternative produced the greatest net return).
6. If a major planning goal is to leave the money under consideration to *heirs*, a deferred annuity is generally a poor choice, because all contract gain will be taxed to that beneficiary as Ordinary Income and the entire annuity value will be includible in the investor's estate, for death tax purposes, with no "step up in basis"[12].

Tax Arguments Offered By Annuity Opponents

A frequent criticism of deferred annuities (usually, but not always, deferred variable annuities) is that they should not be used to fund IRAs or qualified plans. There is no point to doing so, the argument goes, because it "wastes" the tax deferral enjoyed by annuities, because all IRAs and qualified plans get such treatment anyway. Occasionally, one hears the further criticism that such a strategy means "you're paying for tax deferral you're not getting". This is sheer nonsense. *No* annuity imposes *any* charge for tax-deferral. (Whether the charges deferred annuities do impose are worth the benefits the investor gets is a legitimate question, but no purchaser of *any* deferred annuity pays a cent for tax deferral).

The argument that an IRA owner investing in an annuity "wastes" the tax deferral conferred by annuities is not so specious, but it's still nonsense because the "regular annuity rules" of IRC §72 that grant (by implication) tax deferral of undistributed gain to annuity contracts *do not apply* to annuities that fund IRAs or qualified plans. The fundamental flaw of the "wasted deferral" argument is its implicit assumption that the tax treatment that would apply to a particular investment, if held in a "regular" account, is somehow relevant when that same investment is held in a "qualified" account.

A simple example will illustrate the folly of this assumption. If one owns shares of a "small cap growth" stock, or a fund investing in such stocks, and holds those shares for more than one year, one can expect all, or nearly all, gain to be taxed at preferential Long Term Capital Gains rates. But if one holds the same shares in a traditional IRA or qualified plan, those gains, *whenever distributed*, will be taxed at higher Ordinary Income rates. Would any reasonable person conclude from these facts that one should never hold "small cap growth" assets in an IRA or qualified plan because doing so would "waste" the LTCG treatment they would otherwise enjoy? Of course not. Such a conclusion would be foolish - and it is no less foolish when applied to annuities.

Conclusion

The current state of debate about annuities is unfortunate, both for advisors (who are often presented with "educational" materials that are largely polemic) and for consumers (who can hardly be blamed for being confused as to how and when annuities can be appropriate for them – and when and why they might not). Too often, the discussion proceeds from false or shaky assumptions, such as that the M&E charge in a variable annuity is an *investment* expense, rather than what it is (an *insurance* charge for a *risk management* benefit), or that tax deferral is always desirable (even when it requires forfeiting capital gains treatment and a "step up in basis" for beneficiaries).

Even worse than the questionable assumptions is the tendency of many commentators to treat all annuities as though they're more or less alike. In fact, deferred annuities and immediate annuities are very different and are designed to do very different jobs. Similarly, to speak of "annuity costs" as though they apply equally to both fixed and variable contracts is meaningless; variable and "equity index" contracts contain charges and limits on gain that do not appear in traditional fixed annuities.

Annuities and Suitability: Reflections on the State of the Debate

Advisors who offer counsel about annuities need to understand how the various contract types differ and when and how each type can be appropriate. Key to this understanding is a recognition that an annuity, in its most basic sense, is about *income*. This is obvious when the annuity is an immediate one, but it is also true of deferred contracts. The *guarantees* of *minimum income* that are contained in *every* annuity are part of the bundle of benefits the purchaser gets – and part of the annuity's *cost*. If an *assurance* of a *known income* for a *known* period (including one's entire lifetime) is not of concern to the client, the prudent advisor should question whether *any* deferred annuity is appropriate. It may be. The so-called "CD annuities" that offer multi-year interest guarantees (often, for a period extending to the end of the surrender charge period) might well be viewed solely as a *savings* vehicle, comparable to a Certificate of Deposit.

Most deferred annuities, however, are long term instruments. When viewed solely from the standpoint of their ability to produce *capital accumulation*, they suffer from a significant disadvantage, relative to alternatives (such as mutual funds): All distributions will be taxed as Ordinary Income. On the other hand, they enjoy tax deferral. Whether this trade-off will prove advantageous or not to an investor depends upon several factors, the most important of which is Time. The longer the holding period, all other things being equal, the better an annuity will perform, compared to a taxable alternative. If the holding period contains not only a number of years of *accumulation*, but also a period of *distribution*, the annuity often compares favorably to taxable alternatives. And where distributions must persist for the investor's entire lifetime, the annuity really comes into its own. Not only does an extended distribution period increase the benefits of tax deferral, but it brings into play the defining element of any annuity – the *guarantee* that payments will be made as scheduled, *regardless of future changes in interest rates or life expectancy*.

Annuities are all about *income*. If an investor wants and needs *guaranteed income*, an annuity is often a suitable (and sometimes ideal) choice. If he or she does not, its suitability is at least questionable.

1 It is sometimes argued that a particular type of annuity (e.g.: a traditional fixed annuity or an "index annuity") is more a *savings* instrument than an *investment* one. That may be true, but, in the author's opinion, the distinction is not really germane to the issues considered in this article, for which reason, it will not be addressed here.

2 The author concedes that fixed deferred annuities, especially those short-term contracts designed and marketed to compete directly with Certificates of Deposit, could be considered purely "investments" when the purchaser is interested only in the interest rate offered and the deferral of tax liability

3 The *Guaranteed Minimum Accumulation Benefit (GMAB) rider guarantees at least the original principal (and, in some provisions, a minimum return on that principal) at the end of a specified waiting period.*

4 This average figure considers both commissionable and non-commissionable contracts. The average charge for commissionable contracts is higher. The most common annual contract charge, in the author's experience, is 1.4%.

5 The death benefit guaranteed in most fixed deferred annuities is the account balance. There is generally no separate death benefit guarantee, because the guarantee of principal makes one unnecessary.

6 "Separate accounts" (sometimes termed "investment sub-accounts") are invested in pooled equity and/or bond accounts the value of which can, and usually does, change daily. *There is no Safety of Principal or Minimum Guaranteed Return in such accounts.* Amounts invested in the "fixed account" of such contracts are invested in the General Account of the issuing insurer and do enjoy guarantees, both of principal and of a minimum interest rate.

7 It is important to note that only two GLBs guarantee a future *lump sum* value (the GMAB and the "Combination Rider"). The GMIB and GMWB guarantee future values, but only if taken in *installments*.

8 "No-load annuity" is a misnomer. *All* annuities assess some "loads".

9 For example, T. Rowe Price's VA offers only investment accounts managed by T. Rowe Price; Vanguard's VA offers only Vanguard accounts.

10 This is true only when the annuity is owned by a "natural person" (IRC §72(u)) or an entity acting as the "agent of a natural person" (IRC §72(u)(1)).

11 Obviously, the 10% penalty tax (IRC §72(q)), if imposed, will have a significant adverse effect on the annuity's *net* performance. However, if it assumed that distributions will commence after the investors' age 59 ½ and/or be taken over the remaining lifetime of the investor, the exceptions to that penalty offered by IRC §72(q)(2)(A) and/or 72(q)(2)(D) are available.

12 The presence of a Guaranteed Death Benefit (especially if the investor was not insurable at standard rates) would mitigate this general disadvantage of the deferred annuity.

Index

annuities, multiple contracts	27-28
Arkansas Bulletin No.14-2009	90
bright line tests	104, 108, 112
deductibility of loss	28-29
Dodd-Frank Sect 989	78-79, 81
estate taxation	45-48
exchanges	32-34, 82, 86-87, 112
exclusion ratio	62
FINRA Rule 2111	85
FINRA Rule 2230	80, 83, 85
FINRA Rule 2290	84
gifting an annuity	35
guaranteed benefit riders	16, 17-19, 108-109
income taxation	48-64
IRC §67(b)	29
IRC §72	21-22
IRC §72(e)	28, 72-73
IRC §72(h)	59
IRC §72(q)	29-32, 34, 51, 55, 76
IRC §72(s)	45, 48, 52-58, 60-61, 64, 69-72, 74-75
IRC §72(u)	25-26, 69
joint annuities	63-64
market value adjustment	15
mortality credit & risk pooling	7
non-natural persons	25
partial annuitization	38-39
parties to the contract	5
penalties for early distribution	29-30
required minimum distribution	40-41
Rev. Proc. 2008-24	34
Revenue Ruling 2003-76	33
Roth IRA	42
SEC Rule 151A	78
selling an annuity	35
stepped up basis	47
surrender charges	13-14, 27
tax deferral	25
Treas Reg 1.72-2(b)(2)	22
trusts	31-32, 35-38, 68-76